WHEN THE
VISION
IS BIGGER
THAN THE
BUDGET

B Y
J I M
H O L L E Y

Printed by R.H. Boyd Publishing Corporation
Nashville, Tennessee

WHEN THE VISION IS BIGGER THAN THE BUDGET
Copyright © 2008 by R.H. Boyd Publishing Corporation

6717 Centennial Blvd.
Nashville, Tennessee 37209-1017

ISBN 1-58942-469-7

Jim Holley
When the Vision Is Bigger than the Budget

TABLE OF CONTENTS

THE CHALLENGE

Economics and the Church: An Agenda for the Urban Church

There is an impelling personal sense of urgency that time is running out for the Black Church to create a sound economic foundation on which future generations can stand. In order to address this situation, a mission and a purpose-driven mandate should be designed to encourage the Church to stop struggling and to exercise its economic freedom to care for the people who need a helping hand.

For some time now, under the inspiration of God, I have known the words and thoughts that flow from the depths of my heart and reservoir of my mind are the results of the creativity and unlimited wisdom of God. The members and the leaders of the Historic Little Rock Missionary Baptist Church are only instruments—vessels used by God to convey a message of hope to a confused, downtrodden, and hopeless generation that is still wandering in the wilderness almost 150 years after the Emancipation Proclamation. Our present condition and circumstances in no way reflect God's goodness and His purpose for His Church.

"The Spirit of the LORD is upon Me, because He has anointed Me to preach the gospel to the poor; He has sent Me to heal the brokenhearted, to proclaim liberty to the captives and recovery of sight to the blind, to set at liberty those who are oppressed; to proclaim the acceptable year of the LORD." (Luke 4:18-19, NKJV)

For many years I have quietly observed the state of affairs in the Black Church, the Black ministry, Black Church conventions, and Black fraternities and sororities. Essentially, it is about the person, not the people. It's about holding conventions in hotels owned by other ethnic groups and complaining that we don't have our own.

It seems there is no organization helping us, or perhaps we leave it to others to provide "the provision for a vision" and the meaningful self-help initiatives to match that larger vision. It is my humble opinion that the Black Church has outstanding spiritual warrants and will be indicted by the Holy Spirit. This period in history has witnessed the spread of poverty and human suffering, which has left a great and noble people with a sense of hopelessness and economic dependency.

Perhaps what we lack is a godly plan. It was Richard Barber, Sr. who suggested that God gave Moses a compass, "an instrument [that] provides one with consistent direction [and] prevents disorientation and minimizes the possibility of becoming lost." The direction was not determined by Moses or Aaron or Joshua, but by God. Could the reason for forty years of wilderness experience have been to rid the Israelites of their slave mentality and develop a better mental state?

"God's ability, not my ability" should be our maxim. God expects possibilities; He builds on hopes, not on hurts. Receive it, believe it, and you can achieve it. God's delays are not God's denials. When you fail to plan, you plan to fail.

God provided Moses with a compass in the form of a cloud by day and a pillar of fire by night. I think the time is long overdue for the Black Church to develop, with God's help, a business-based compass in order to implement an economic agenda that brings about measurable progress for each generation.

Have you not agonized over our dependence on other groups for practically all of our goods and services? Visualize the following scenario: You are awakened in the morning by a clock made by Westinghouse or General Electric. You crawl out the bed with sheets made by Cannon Mills. You walk across tile or carpet from the Armstrong Cork Company. You go into the bathroom where you turn on a faucet or shower control made by American Standard Company. You lather with soap made by Proctor and Gamble. You step out of the shower and use a Cannon Mills towel to dry your body. You shave using a Gillette™ or Schick™ razor. You brush your teeth with Colgate™ and use Scope™ mouthwash. You continue your ritual by using a Faberge deodorant stick and Johnson and Johnson Soft Sheen™, followed by Dudley or Pro-Line Hair Spray. You step into your Hanes underwear, Brooks Brother suit, Gucci or Florsheim shoes, put on your Stetson hat, pick up your briefcase made by China Leather Company, and walk out to your General Motors vehicle in the driveway and drive off, leaving a Japanese Toyota Camry™ in the driveway for your spouse who is inside hurriedly repeating the similar routine. You drive away humming, "We shall overcome." And if by chance you meet your fate during the day while on the job, you are laid to rest in a casket from the Casket Company and your flowers from FTD.

How long, O God? How long?

Please understand that 10 percent of the population owns 90 percent of the wealth. Based on what we have seen from these greedy tycoons, we can expect poverty, homelessness, and unemployment to continue to plague the underclass in our communities.

As foreign business interests continue to acquire American business enterprises at an alarming rate, and American corporate interests continue to seek slave labor markets abroad in their pursuit of greater profits, the overall interests of African Americans and other minorities of this nation are not being well-served. This situation presents a grim picture, but all is not lost. These conditions provide us with a challenge and an opportunity: a challenge to change some of the past economic wrongs and an opportunity to develop a compass of our own.

It is my humble belief that there are many individuals like Moses in our church community. Like the prophet, modern leaders should not seek permission from the congregation to lead; that mandate comes from God.

Often, the reality is that we, as leaders, are afraid to step out of our comfort zones. We are afraid to step out of the box and seek God's face with our faith.

The Rev. Dr. Martin Luther King, Jr. had a dream, and I am suggesting we move from the dream to a vision and trust God for the provision.

Let me suggest to you that one of the biggest problems we face as a people is that we do not control our destiny or our financial resources. Should we not be concerned that our insurance premiums and the money we deposit in banks, savings and loans associations, and pension programs provide little, if any, investment returned to our own communities?

I remember when the South African apartheid system dominated 28 million Black South Africans. American Blacks, through the American financial system, made $7 billion in loans to South Africa. Indirectly, we were funding the economic and political slavery of our own people.

Trust me when I tell you that the economic destiny of African Americans rests upon the strength, commitment, and unfulfilled potential of the Black Church. The Black Church as an institution has played a primary leadership role in the progress and development of Black America. It has no doubt been our "bridge over troubled waters," from slavery until this very moment.

In a time when government entitlements to the poor and community groups are decreasing, it is imperative for the Church to assume an even greater responsibility for finding solutions to some of the social and economic problems plaguing our communities. This situation presents an opportunity for the Christian community to take the initiative and to assume an active role in developing and implementing an economic program that will directly address the employment and business enterprise development needs for our community.

As church leaders and assorted "pew warmers," we are collectively challenged to demonstrate that we can influence the destiny of our own community. But to achieve a greater degree of economic standing and control, we must develop a far more financially-based solution to accomplish any solid and lasting progress.

Now African Americans are facing that last frontier, and this may be our last chance to eliminate a major barrier to participation in the economic and financial mainstream of America.

It seems as if every ethnic group sees Black America as a viable market except ourselves. We are a $500 billion consumer market. The Black Church must accept its economic muscle. It is so easy for us to complain about our economic failures while we commit economic suicide. Generations to come will never forgive us for failing to seize the moment and opportunity. This task does not have to be done collectively; it can be done church by church and neighborhood by neighborhood. We can strengthen our communities that have been plagued by double-digit unemployment, economic deprivation, and a sense of hopelessness.

For decades we have taught and preached in our churches, state conventions, and national conventions that "we serve a great and mighty God"—and we do serve an all-powerful Creator. We have been taught that God supplies all our needs and gives us the desires of our hearts. The cattle on a thousand hills belong to Him. All of these axioms are true.

The tragedy is that all we do is to observe passively the poverty, unemployment, male imprisonment, and terrible health conditions suffered by our people. We are stepping stones for others but stumbling blocks to each other. Why are we so determined to maintain the poverty mentality?

"No one can save us from us but us." After all, with few exceptions, other ethnic groups have no vested interest in our economic freedom and independence.

Introduction

EMBARKING UPON A BUSINESS TO SUPPORT THE OUTREACH MINISTRY

During the last several years, federal and state governments have dismantled many programs for the poor and senior citizens. New political alliances have emerged that reflect a changed consensus about governmental responsibility for the support given to various marginalized groups. Whereas at one time the debate had centered on the extent of support for the poor, the elderly, homeless, and other at-risk groups, now the debate has shifted to whether or not the federal and state governments even have such an obligation. This transformation of thought resulted, in large part, in a swift turn from long-established policies and programs. The loss of the funds these programs previously provided to urban communities has inevitably created a strain on the local church and other faith-based organizations and institutions. Today, whereas White churches are often prosperous and occasionally even possess endowments, the Black Church is often impoverished. Most urban churches depend solely upon the congregation for their money. In fact, such churches rely almost exclusively upon the weekly collection. If a snowstorm, rainstorm, or as in recent history, a hurricane stops people from coming to church, the church loses its offering and, thus, its main source of income. When the offering is lost, so is the support for important outreach ministries.

Historic Little Rock Missionary Baptist Church is no exception to this pattern. Like many other churches, it has found itself in the familiar role of providing for the poor, the elderly, the homeless, and other similarly disadvantaged groups. In fact, such people are drawn to Little Rock because it offers food, shelter, clothing, and other services once provided primarily by governmental agencies. Little Rock's role as an auxiliary force to governmental programs has become essential to the continued livelihood of many people. The church continues to grow numerically, but with fewer monetary resources. In fact, an increasing number of church members now

1

require the human services that were formerly funded by tax money. The church must now subsidize these services with weekly tithes and offerings, but this weekly income cannot begin to make up for the loss of government support. In our case, we face a $7,000 weekly shortfall in the income needed to sustain our outreach programs. Our collections at services would have to increase 70 percent in order to match the needs of the church's programs. As pastor, I face this crisis with no formal business training. Thus far, current seminary educational programs do not address business matters as they pertain to churches.

To secure our future, we at the Historic Little Rock Missionary Baptist Church began to assess our growth and our outreach ministry, and we discovered that monetary support for outreach had not grown in proportion with the church's membership. The church had grown from 43 to 3,030 members, but 63 percent of the membership was on a fixed income or had no income at all; youth and young adults comprised 17 percent of the membership; and only 20 percent of the membership tithed regularly. The proclamation of the Word and the work of church personnel had increased our numbers but not the income needed for our budget. As the population grew, so did the needs of the people and the amount of financial support needed to carry out this ministry.

- The senior citizens needed support in health care and were raising grandchildren who had been neglected or abandoned.
- The youth needed programs to provide the services that the public schools could not totally provide.
- The young adults wanted higher education and/or job development, job creation, and job placement.

Quite simply, the separation of our parishioners from society could be measured, in part, by the separation from the economic resources that were once available to them.

Pastors and other church leaders in this new millennium must be aware of these circumstances. We must meet the diverse challenges that congregations experience, while at the same time addressing their legitimate needs. Without a new solution, churches in urban America may have to shut their doors or become "dead" churches with no real or substantive ministries. The Church needs to address and solve this crisis.

At the heart of this change is the need to restructure our relationship to parts of the culture that have traditionally been quite different from the vision of the Church. Particularly, we need to understand how the church weaves its presence into a society characterized by a complex business structure. We need to understand the nature of business enterprise not only for financial support but also because business organization is far more porous and adaptable than we have traditionally imagined. In so doing, we will ultimately change the very fabric of ministry support in our communities.

However, the problems of outreach ministries are compounded by many churches' lack of prior planning in order to meet present community needs. The most difficult challenge in ministry is to see pain and to know that you are the medicine for people who cannot afford the cure. Pastors and religious leaders must now realize that the future Church and its mission and ministry are intricately tied to our ability to go beyond traditional means of support. We can no longer expect our efforts to be fueled solely by a desire of the people to feel good about the ministry, especially when these same people are jobless, illiterate, homeless, and hungry. We especially need to find new means of support for our youth, who are often jailed or not employed.

One way we found support for our ministries at Little Rock was to start Country Preacher Foods, Inc., which has enabled us to build on Scriptural principles to provide resources for the Church to meet this financial crisis in our outreach ministries. Country Preacher Foods, Inc. has proven successful for the ministry of Little Rock. We have a staff of four and projected business earnings of $5 million. These earnings are expected to increase over the next three years. Our product line has grown from one to seventeen items. We developed a business with a unique product, a business that generates finances and increases resources for the outreach programs that would have otherwise been eliminated due to a lack of financial resources. (An extensive description of Country Preacher Foods, Inc. follows in a later chapter.)

This concept of merging ministry with business establishes a vision for the outreach ministry of the 21st-century Church and works toward a theology of community development and business enterprise. In reality, we are faced with the challenge of gaining a greater understanding of the relationship between capitalism and ministry. It is important that the 21st-century Church, its pastors and leaders, develop the spirit of entrepreneurship. We must all admit that carrying out the Church's mission has become more complex. As spelled out before, government cutbacks, changing societal beliefs regarding the responsibility of all citizens for the poor, and the necessary new roles for the Church have forced us to think about how the Church operates in the world. The ministry of the Church *to* the world is a ministry based *in* the world, a world whose economic foundations can no longer be ignored. Given the context of the urban ministry crisis, we must ultimately strive to make the business of Christ a reality for the Church. God still has treasures in some of the most unfamiliar places.

For some time, I have considered how business enterprise could be adapted to the ministry of the Church. Part of the answer has to do with being driven by necessity, but the other part of the answer involves redefining the role of profit and reaching into the White corporate world and changing their racial beliefs. Meeting with White corporate America on common ground allows us to handcuff them with their own rhetoric. If they believe that affirmative action should be dismantled and that people on welfare should be self-reliant, then they should appreciate a church with an entrepreneurial spirit for two reasons: for profit and for the consistency with their own vision of what constitutes the community. Business practices will begin to cross racial lines as long as everyone makes money—including the retailer, manufacturer, and distributor—then the energy that was being used to limit others is now freed to serve all people.

The tension that results from reconciling business reports, bottom lines, gross sales, and projected profits exactly mirrors the experience of the Church in adapting to a world where the money lenders are driven from the Temple but not out of the marketplace. It is a difficult process, but one that must be acted upon if the 21st-century Church hopes to bring the Word to a very weary world.

Chapter 1

FROM AN ANTIQUATED MINISTRY TO A MODERN MINISTRY

It does not take a rocket scientist to realize that urban America is in a state of crisis. Urban leaders, and many scholars, acknowledge that our churches and neighborhoods are experiencing an unprecedented social, moral, cultural, and economic breakdown. It seems that there are no sure answers or solutions. To make matters worse, even suburban America does not know the cause of the unraveling of the moral fabric of our cities and neighborhoods. While we have traditions that make visible these losses, we inhabit a new world where our traditional solutions do not always work. Our response to the world must change because the world itself is different.

The Urban Church must address this crisis and become a "beacon of light in a community of blight." The rebuilding, renewal, and empowerment of the 21st-century Church in the community is reflected in our mission to do the business of Christ in the city. For any church to survive, it must acknowledge that there is a need for the community to thrive and to have, as John Perkins would say, "Safe streets, schools that educate, a viable economy, wholesome recreational and social activities, be engaged in political affairs, and reflect spiritual and ethical leadership."[1] There is agreement within our communities that moral fiber, self-determination, and self-reliance are threads that hold together the fabric of a community. The primary problem that faces the Church is how to nurture these elements of a positive community and enable the integrity and character of people to shape their own destiny. We can achieve this by engaging in a trustworthy relationship with the people in the community and by beginning to meet their needs. John Perkins introduced this idea of beginning with "people's felt need" in 1986.[2] The major distinction that the 21st-century Church must incorporate is to address these "felt

5

needs" through the enlargement of community outreach ministries. Additionally, there must be a specifically Biblical approach to the community that strengthens economic development. By bringing the Church into contact with the forces of economics that influence almost all of contemporary life, we strengthen our influence, not only in the local community but in the larger culture as well.

OLD WINE IN NEW SKINS

It is often an arduous task to serve the larger community as Christ would have us to do. Often belief statements promulgated by congregations that are resistant to change reflect heightened anxiety at the prospect of a new approach to ministry. Like many churches, at the Historic Little Rock Missionary Baptist Church there was a general feeling that the focus of the Church should be the salvation of souls, not saving money and certainly not participating in business enterprises. Many felt that if we as a church decided to support this type of Christian economic development strategy, we could not afford it. This kind of thinking usually unveils the fears of cautious, yet caring people who attempt to take the "old wine" of outdated approaches and apply those to the "new wineskins" of a new day. The thought of moving parishioners from the comfort of their nests into unknown territory is for some pastors simply frightening.

There are two traditions that usually stand in the way of change in the modern Church. The first tradition is that the Church is a refuge from the turmoil of the world. The second tradition believes the Church should not involve itself in anything that remotely resembles the world, in particular, something as wicked—they presume—as making money. The dilemma is that to enter the world of capitalism is a risky undertaking, and it is equally frightening to abandon the familiar Church world and everything that it teaches.

What is the Church supposed to do? This is a difficult question to answer because for years our churches seemed to be interested only in "meeting and eating." From all indications, the traditional thinking has been to emphasize the proclamation of the Word and to base success on how many people were in attendance on Sundays. Many of our churches have been interested only in just paying the bills and maintaining themselves as religious social clubs.

Because federal, state, and local governments have all but abandoned their responsibilities to the least among us, the Church must be proactive and creative in supporting these new undertakings. The goals of empowering people and serving our communities mean that we must seek to go beyond that which is comfortable and move to what is most important. In all honesty, as a pastor, I too have in the past contributed to the spiritual and directional slump of the Historic Little Rock Missionary Baptist Church. For years, I was more interested in building the numbers and less interested in teaching the Word. My belief was that more members meant more resources, and more resources meant more support for the ministry. It did not happen that way. For some reason, the profile of the church was static and only attracted more of the same. Increasing compassion for the poor and the preaching of the Social Gospel often draw more members to the fold that come to be served. While many urban churches are growing numerically, their economic profiles are not changing. Therefore, the needs become greater, while the income of those same churches increases only slightly or remains the same.

According to the history of the Historic Little Rock Missionary Baptist Church, from 1972 through 1976 the church moved courageously and faithfully from its humble beginnings in a house basement to a location on the east side of Detroit. The new building was formerly a Lutheran church with a seating capacity of 350. The church reflected a highly spiritual and biblically-motivated membership during this period. Later the congregation moved four more times and called a total of five pastors to this ministry. However, the church growth never reached more than 350 members; it actually dropped as low as 43 members at one time.

Although the members were good people, they had developed a complacency that didn't respond to the changes in how the needs of the community should be met. The members were satisfied with their particular community. This generation had grown up together, not just in worship but also in the formation of their faith. The church was made up of blue-collar workers and one professional—a principal in the local high school. All the eyes and ears of the congregation were upon him for vision and direction. The ministry was in a position like that of the ship whose progression was limited and survival in question due to adverse conditions. The conditions were such that, according to the Apostle Paul, the sailors "prayed for daylight" (Acts 27:29, NIV). The community of the church, albeit insulated from some of the economic forces of the world surrounding it, had to be extended beyond the walls of the church and into the larger world of the problems that beset the poor, the elderly, the sick, and the homeless—basically all those who Christ has called the Church to serve.

By the time I became pastor, the membership had declined to fewer than one hundred members. The ministry during the years of 1972 through 1978 centered on increasing the church membership from 100 to 900 members. The weekly offering during this time increased from a few hundred dollars to $3,000 per week. With increased revenues, the leadership of the church was also able to purchase a house, three other properties, a bus, and a van. The church was remodeled and a baptismal pool and additional pews were installed. The mortgage was also paid off, in addition to a $96,000 loan for an addition to the church building.

This new church was financed by one of the banks in the community that had confidence in our ability to grow and invest in the area. Seven hundred church members moved to this beautiful Neo-Gothic edifice with a 1,560-person seating capacity. The new building housed 27 meeting rooms, a nursery, day care facilities, a banquet room, men and women's lounges, and a gym. Moving to this central geographic location increased the church's opportunity to serve not only the church membership but also the larger community. The purpose of the church was focused on filling the seats, multiplying and prospering, to fulfilling the evangelistic mission of the Church, and to identifying the goals and objectives that would vitalize the faith of each member.

In spite of all of the advances for the physical space, these good people still had no apparent vision. Moreover, they had not been challenged to create or follow a vision. The board of directors was wonderful but fearful: fearful because they sensed the Lord had given me, as the pastor, the vision. Yet, they needed faith, not sight, to see the vision as well. Consequently, like many well-meaning but traditional church boards, the board of directors understood its ministry to be "keepers of the aquarium and not fishers of men." For this board of directors, education was a dream, not a reality; the ministry of Jesus was worship, not service.

The Historic Little Rock Missionary Baptist Church is situated in a poor area of Detroit and has a membership that was once worship-oriented instead of service-oriented. As a new pastor, I had the responsibility of revealing to the congregation why God had brought us to this particular location. It was then and still is my belief that our congregation is in this location for the purpose of rebuilding the community. In response to this vision, the membership originally replied, "This is a beautiful church; let's not let outsiders tear it up." We were in danger of becoming an enclave within our own city, a sort of spiritual suburb within the city's boundaries.

According to Eugene Rivers, this kind of attitude within urban America is a product of a generation of poor Blacks who "may reach the end of this century in an...inferior position to their ancestors, who entered the century in the shadow of formal slavery. Unable to see a more rational future through the eyes of faith, they lack the hope that sustained their forebears. Lacking hope, they experience...social death."[3]

The Apostle Paul was no stranger to the lack of hope causing social and economic death of the inner city. When he wrote a letter to Christians in the capital city of Rome, he realized that the current situation did not look good for the people of God. Politically, the Roman Emperor Nero proved to be one of the staunchest opponents of Christianity while he was on the throne. Christians were subjected to the cruelest punishments the human mind could imagine. Poverty and crime were rampant. Carroll Felton points out that "one could hardly walk down the Via Appia without being solicited, propositioned, or mugged."[4] Yet, Paul wrote of hope when he stated, "Against all hope, Abraham in hope believed and so became the father of many nations...he did not waver through unbelief regarding the promise of God, but was strengthened in his faith and gave glory to God, being fully persuaded that God had power to do what he had promised" (Rom. 4:18, 20-21, NIV).

The hope of the urban churches rests ultimately on the power of God and His love for those in the city. Dealing with a generation that has lost faith and hope and has succumbed to social rejection and despair should be enough to spur the Church into bringing the Gospel of hope to the inner city. As John Perkins states:

> Our nation's cities are in a crisis. But in every crisis there is opportunity. I believe that this crisis is an opportunity for us, the church, to step forward and lead the way in restoring the inner city by bringing the physical presence of God into the city. I believe that the church has the opportunity to pioneer a way of life whereby our nation itself can experience a new birth.[5]

There are times when the areas around our churches appear to have made progress; however, we must not forget that often old memories and past thoughts are still lingering in the minds and spirits of the faith community. The challenge for the 21st-century Church is to find a way to re-weave the unraveled neighborhood into a quality place for all people. It is critical that we do not become discouraged simply because past social experiments have yielded nothing. At least we know what does not work, even though we may not be sure what will work. Our task is to bring our message to the world through our actions; through action, we turn our back on despair. There is great value in being a good neighbor or citizen whose life is modeled on a loving God. There should be no question that God would find this behavior acceptable, for God asks us the question, "Who is your neighbor?"

At the end of 1993 and the beginning of 1994, I, as pastor, began to question our ministry's calling and the calling of the minister. If the expectations of the church and the surrounding community are not as high as the minister's, then perhaps there is a spiritual disconnect. I have never questioned the fact God placed me in the pastorate, but the question of whether or not I was fulfilling the mission of the ministry gnawed at my conscience. Many, in order to avoid confronting their consciences, simply seek another assignment with another congregation. However, if we are certain of our placement and calling, and rest assured in God's design for us, the following questions still remain:

1. How can we convince the congregation that regular tithing and offerings are necessary and righteous?

2. How can we direct our attention to the broader needs
    ensuring our children's education and the developmen,
    surrounding community, over and above tithing and offe.

At Little Rock, our church records revealed there were app.oxi-
mately forty-two students in our congregation who were enrolled in
community colleges and universities. Many urban students lack financial support for college. We must admit that while many of our
churches collect infrequent and token offerings in an attempt to subsidize the college education of our students, what is collected is in
effect just a drop in the bucket for the student. Additional concerns
include how long our congregations will remain patient and the problem of wearing the church's budget too thin. I started to wonder if a
business could be created that would enable the church to generate
enough revenue to support the students' continuing education, as well
as other requests for help.

On Christmas Day, 1994, Little Rock's answer to this dilemma
came in the form of a for-profit company called Country Preacher
Foods, Inc. This business was created to support a non-profit organization called the Children in Progress (CHIP) Foundation. Country
Preacher Foods, Inc. was established to create a product that was mar-
ketable and profitable for the purpose of generating financial resources
for the CHIP Foundation. The foundation, in turn, would support
the ministries of helping the homeless, providing student scholarships,
and working with community economic development projects.

The Country Preacher Company is a growing multi-million dollar
corporation that supports ministries that tithes and offerings are not
in a position to sustain. The vision to focus on education, scholarships, the homeless, and the development of a small shopping mall
only became a reality because of a shift in thinking to merge business
enterprise and ministry. In addition, Country Preacher Foods, Inc. has
been able to provide urban families with new housing units in the
community by funding the Historic Little Rock Baptist Church Non-
Profit Housing Corporation.

The charge for the forward-thinking church seeking to uplift its
community is to face the reality that the community is coming apart.
In large measure, this is because of neglect and a lack of creativity and

imagination within many churches. Given the fact that healthy communities tend to produce healthy families, the Church should promote and create programs that support traditional values.[6] Perkins reminds us, "Families are as vulnerable without stable communities as communities are without stable families. Without interconnected neighbors functioning as living ligatures to hold neighborhoods together, disintegration occurs."[7] It is my hope that our church's model, whether implicitly or explicitly, will help stop the larger church community from unknowingly promoting its own demise.

The 21st-century Church must understand that the historic mission of the Church is to be proactively armed with love, to infiltrate every stratum of society, and to transform fallen people by empowering them through the power of the Holy Spirit. While attempting to allow the body of Christ to become the enclave of like-minded friends, the results of many churches' efforts have provided a protective haven from the daily bombardment of destructive values. Nevertheless, engagement, not withdrawal, has always been the operative word of Jesus' disciples. The decree of Jesus in Luke 10:27 to "love your neighbor as yourself" remains fundamental (NIV).

The church must not be measured by the number of members but by the quantity and quality of its ministries. Church ministries must empower people through education, jobs, and property ownership. The possibilities exist and the challenges call out, yet the cooperation is halting. As the people of God, we cannot wait for a road map before going forward. I personally have come to learn the Lord works when you commit yourself to a venture in which God reveals Himself to you.

A NEW MODEL FOR A NEW DAY

The need for the Church to have a new operating model is simply because the Urban Church is facing unprecedented demands in a time of unprecedented governmental deficits. Therefore, since God has not relinquished the Church from its mission of meeting needs, a new method of ministry must be developed. This model should have at its core several key elements: (1) development of a Biblically-based community outreach vision for the Urban Church and community; (2) development of a non-profit organization to provide an educational foundation for opportunity; and (3) implementation of a strategy to develop a for-profit enterprise to support the local church's community outreach ministries. In this way, the church can be a role model for Christian community economic development that will support ministries whose resources are limited.

There is a Biblical basis for the whole concept of focusing on the business of Christ in the city. This business involves meeting the needs of the people, spreading the Gospel in the highways and byways, and being your brother's keeper. Many churches attempt to establish ministries to reach out and address the needs of the community; however, their efforts are often blocked by lack of funds. In Matthew 16:13-19, Jesus authorizes the Church to tear down the spiritual stronghold of hell which has been established in our inner cities. In Matthew 28:18-20, Jesus commissions the Church to make disciples of all nations. This is not to say it is impossible to do ministry in the inner city through organizations not tied to the local church. However, as Glen Kehrein argues convincingly, "We do believe that spiritual needs will be best addressed by the organization that is tied to a church."[8]

THE THEOLOGY OF BUSINESS

We do not have to dig too deeply into the Bible to find references that offer strong analogies to community development and local partnering to enable empowerment. Our desire is not that others might be relieved while you are hard-pressed, but that there might be the sort of equality that allows us to turn our energy toward the spiritual life. Paul's second letter to the Corinthians gives us hope: "At the present time your plenty will supply what they need, so that in turn their plenty will supply what you need. Then there will be equality" (2 Cor. 8:14, NIV). Paul recognizes that suffering and the desire for more interfere with spirituality. They also divide the community of believers. All the believers were one in heart and mind. No one claimed that any of his possessions was his own, but they all shared everything they had. With great power, the Apostles continued to testify to the resurrection of the Lord Jesus, and much grace was upon them all. As the writer of Acts said, "There were no needy persons among them" (4:34, NIV). In the story of the fishes and the loaves, as recorded in John 6, Jesus fed about five thousand individuals with only two small fish and five barley loaves. Whereas the other Gospel writers do not mention where the fish and loaves originated from, John tells us that a boy was found by Andrew who had these things in his possession. Even though the boy had provisions, Andrew wondered, "How far will they go among so many?" (v. 9, NIV). Andrew and the remaining disciples' vision was limited. Two fish and five loaves of bread could barely feed the Twelve. However, Jesus took what little was offered and satisfied the crowd's hunger. John's pericope shows us that no matter how meager our resources might seem, God can multiply them to fulfill the needs of others. As the Apostle Paul wrote in his epistle to the Philippians, "Each of you should look not only to your own interests, but also to the interests of others" (2:4, NIV).

More and more of our churches and community leaders are discovering that empowerment is the most effective solution for the spiritual and economic development of the poor. The more insecure and unsafe our cities become, the more middle-class residents run for their lives. Are we going to leave the city empty of any Christian presence? The future of America begins with Christian development programs that are willing to stand with the people. What price are we willing to pay as a faith community? Salt and light go where others dare not travel. The people of God must stand among those with the very needs we are commanded to fill, and we must do it with the same mercy and love found in the model of Christ.

1 John M. Perkins, *Beyond Charity: The Call to Christian Community Development* (Grand Rapids: Baker Book House, 1993), 80.
2 Ibid, 18.
3 Eugene F. Rivers, "On the Responsibility of Intellectuals in the Age of Crack," *Boston Review*, (September-October, 1992), 14.
4 Carroll M. Felton, Jr., *The Care of Souls in the Black Church: A Liberation Perspective* (New York: Martin Luther King Fellows Press, 1980), 37.
5 Perkins, *Beyond Charity*, 58
6 Ibid, 88.
7 Ibid, 88.
8 Glen Kehrein and Raleigh Washington. *Breaking Down the Walls: A Model for Reconciliation in an Age of Racial Strife* (Chicago: Moody Press, 1993), 17.

Chapter 2

THE GREAT DIVIDE

Most of the people in our country who are being trained in the capital-intensive, information-based, service-oriented jobs of the present and future are White. Given that Blacks are disproportionately represented among those who suffer from the neglect of our public schools, the failure to train our young for a productive future reflects itself most acutely in the Black experience. Most of the people aspiring to succeed through higher education in the city where Historic Little Rock Missionary Baptist Church is located have been hurt by cuts in Pell Grants, guaranteed student loans, and other forms of aid for post-secondary education. Twenty-five percent of our young people who could have gone to college a few years ago have no opportunity to do so today. It seems that the prevailing economic theory in America strikes the Black community with three destructively mistaken assumptions: (1) the poor have too much money; (2) the rich have too little money; and (3) our problems in the inner city can be solved by building more prisons and sports stadiums.

The quality of life in any society may be determined not by how it treats its rich, able, and affluent citizens but by how it treats the weak, struggling, and infirm among us. When we use this barometer to gauge the depth of our compassion, we cannot help but painfully conclude the springs of mercy within us have closed up and the springs of sympathy within us have dried up. If our cities have become deserts, then the cities are victims of a spiritual drought that will not quench the thirst for education among our children.

We have to be careful that we do not get so caught up in "having church" that we forget to be "the Church." We can become so excited about the formal worship service that we forget to render service.

When you get right down to it, there is no real worship to God if we fail to serve humanity. In *The Crisis in Black and Black*, Dr. Earl Ofari Hutchinson points out that "...the crisis in black and black is profound and troubling. It has confused and jaded some blacks as to what to do. It has caused despair among others. It has triggered hostility and conflict between still others. What must be done is not to argue over solutions but be productive to overcome the crisis."[1]

This is what the Church should have in mind as it begins to make some effort to support outreach ministries. The solution that most effectively reaches past the consequences of government abandonment of the needy is education. There are other problems that come out of decisions we cannot control. In education, however, there is a means for building a community of young people who can create better consequences for the world. The benefits of having these educated young people return to our communities would result in stronger families and stronger communities—places where faith would flourish. Education allows us to create positive results rather than suffer the consequences of an increasingly selfish culture.

Several years ago, requests for financial support from members and friends of members for educational resources were received in large numbers at our church. The Scholarship Committee was requested to survey these inquiries and report back to me. The survey information was to include the nature of the request, demographic data, and whether the requests were from church members or their immediate families. A few weeks later, I met with the Scholarship Committee. The reported data was so appalling that it left all of us distraught and near despair. There were eighty-seven financial requests from students in forty-three universities and colleges. Sixty-seven requests were from members of families active in the church. The requests ranged from three hundred to several thousand dollars, and the desires ranged from books to tuition assistance to fees for graduation. Several of the request letters were read to me, and the one that caught my attention most was the following, which read: "You are the reason I am in school; your life-sharing experiences and your belief that education is the passport from poverty to prosperity."[2] This letter burned into my heart, and I knew any rejection of these requests would have a devastating impact on these young scholars. To reject these requests would cast the Church in the same mold as all of the other social forces that had turned their backs on Black intelligence, Black discipline, and a future created by the strength of educated Black women and men.

The Scholarship Committee suggested more fundraising programs, special offerings, and perhaps a carnival for education. These were fine suggestions, but these efforts would not raise enough revenue to cover the price of providing these aspiring scholars with hope and a certainty of opportunity. I remembered reading in *Acts of Faith*, "Buried deep in the earth are precious diamonds. In order to get to them, however, we must dig and dig deep. It is not the digging; it is the pressure that makes diamonds."[3] The pressure was on; the work needed to concentrate on saving these eighty-seven students for now and perhaps several thousands more in the future.

The Gospel of Mark relates, "And one of the multitude answered and said, Master, I have brought unto thee my son, which hath a dumb spirit; And wheresoever he taketh him, he teareth him: and he foameth, and gnasheth with his teeth, and pineth away: and I spake to thy disciples that they should cast him out; and they could not" (9:17-18, KJV). The man in this passage signifies a Church without power. It is important that our youth who make requests to further their education do not see the Church as powerless to help them in their financial dilemmas. Every church should remain sensitive and feel the burden of its youth when their cry for help is for something as basic as a post-secondary education. The letter I received reminded me of being responsible for instilling in this young person the desire to obtain an education and a way out of potential poverty and chaos. Education gives our youth an articulate voice in the world—a voice that can serve the family and the community and that can speak in tones informed by Christian values. Extending our mission into the world means extending our presence into the world.

In a prayerful mode and with spiritual direction, I fasted and prayed for three days with the intention of a seven-day fast. However, on the fourth day, the *Wall Street Journal* reported the Famous Amos Cookie Company, two years out of bankruptcy, was sold for a whopping $55 million. In the middle of my own fast, it dawned on me that somebody out there was eating cookies in this country. With all of these cookies being eaten, would there be a chance for another minority cookie company? If I could talk to Wally "Famous" Amos, I could get his advice on making and marketing cookies in a national market.

Wally Amos agreed to meet with me on April 7, 1994, in Honolulu, Hawaii. For several hours, we talked and shared cookie production strategies. As a result, I came away from this meeting feeling encouraged and full of useful information from a professional businessman. But the convergence of forces that were leading the church to a new strategy continued to build.

During the return flight on Northwest Airlines from Honolulu to Detroit, I perused *World Magazine*. It was obvious there were no minority vendors in the list of foods served on Northwest flights. Upon arriving back at the church, I sent communication to Northwest to request a meeting to discuss a cookie concept for the purpose of generating income for our education outreach. Personnel at Northwest Airlines were interested and asked me to meet with them at the Detroit Metropolitan Airport. Northwest Airlines flew in a procurement officer from Minneapolis, Minnesota, and a chef from New York. An agreement on price structures and all the particulars were to be outlined in a departmental communication.

This was an exciting time and a tremendous opportunity because it marked the beginning of a journey. But it was a journey not only to a new location, the transformation of our community was involved as well. We had to come to the table of economics to realize that promise. In this case, it was at the table of Northwest Airlines. Northwest indicated that, if the church wanted their business, it would be through a pilot program. The size of the contract and its duration were precisely limited, and the church had to demonstrate its discipline and skill. My role as pastor took on duties I had scarcely imagined. My tasks were specific: (1) find a cookie company and make sure it could meet Northwest's specifications for taste, packaging, quality, and the meeting of deadlines; and (2) limit costs to thirteen cents per cookie.

A company named Awrey Bakery, considered one of the oldest and best bakeries in the state of Michigan, agreed to manufacture the cookies provided that we could create a unique recipe and successfully negotiate the price. The recipe came from a church family member with modifications being made by the bakery. The price to package, bake, and deliver was twelve and one-half cents per cookie. That meant only half a penny per cookie would be the profit, thus, we were advised to abandon this project. However, our project team became aware that to do business with a major airline such as Northwest at a rate of 17 thousand cookies per day could be eventually leveraged as if the profit were a dollar per cookie. This is called "leverage marketing." It is a strategy that is especially productive when you are undercapitalized and at risk of losing an account altogether.

This was the beginning of Country Preacher Foods, Inc. This represented the first contract, the first business for the church, and a way to support the outreach ministries of the church. Ultimately, it was a pivotal move for any faith-based institution to do business with a company as large as Northwest Airlines. The project at this point was to finance the cookie ingredients, packaging, and labeling. The Awrey Baking Company agreed to have the plates made for the logo and supply the paper and materials for the packaging. The capital investment would be returned to the company upon delivery. These efforts would represent Awrey Bakery Company's way of giving back to the community. This is how the profit could be so small at the beginning of this particular venture. The thought was that with market creation and sales volume the investment of the Awrey Bakery Company would be paid for, and another penny could be added to the profit side of the ledger.

L. Douglas Wilder, the former governor of Virginia, once said in a speech at the Economic Club of Detroit, "The thing is to never deal yourself out...opt for the best possible hand. Play with verve and sometimes with abandon, but at all times with calculation."[4]

The key to establishing a business presence in the world is to focus on the things you can ultimately control. Successful outcomes are not simply to be measured in terms of profit. For the 21st-century Church to do business in the city, success must also be measured in multiple layers that supply the monetary foundation for the outreach ministries of the church. In the case of the Historic Little Rock Missionary Baptist Church, the outcome of our first business venture would give us control of our finances and that, in turn, would give us control of our outreach. Ultimately, this control of our outreach would grant control of the educational lives of the intelligent students who sought admission to colleges and universities. The students stood at these doors barred from admission—not by the presence of police guns and dogs—but by an entity just as dangerous: the absence of financial resources. Our initial contract with Northwest Airlines began to open those college and university doors. And through those doors, we opened a new world to the church.

1 Earl Ofari Hutchinson, *The Crisis in Black and Black* (Los Angeles: Middle Passage Press, 1998), 177.

2 Severson Welch to Reverend Jim Holley, 23 November 1994, transcript in the hand of Rev. Jim Holley. Personal letter.

3 Iyanla Vanzant, *Acts of Faith: Daily Meditations for People of Color* (New York: Simon & Schuster, 1996), 13.

4 L. Douglas Wilder written to the Economic Club of Detroit. Speech, 17 March 1992.

Chapter 3

THE MANTLE OF COMMUNITY DEVELOPMENT

The challenges for the members of urban American churches include unemployment, inadequate educational opportunities, substandard housing, desolation, and neighborhood blight. The lack of access to adequate healthcare, destruction of the family, and unrelenting poverty, as well as drug addiction, despair, and apathy all test our faith in the world. The world no longer chooses to look upon the suffering masses and provide them with help. It is a world that has left the Church to serve as the last bastion of hope for the least of our fellow men. The immense burden that proved too difficult for the conscience of our government and other organizations has now fallen upon our shoulders. We have to remember what was once accomplished when Christlike acts sprang from the subversive teaching of the early Church (see Acts 4:32-35). We must also undertake our outreach in a directly Christian fashion to achieve what our faith demands.

There is no mystery about how government can be a positive influence on the social and economic framework of society. When you create opportunities for decent housing and health care and provide education and training, you help people move out of poverty. When kids attend quality preschool programs, they do better in school and have higher rates of college attendance, after-graduation employment, and lower rates of teen pregnancy and criminal activity. Quality job training programs generate a more productive workforce and more stable communities. The treasury receives back $4 or $5 for every $1 that it invests in skills training programs. There is no mystery in these facts. The real mystery is the reluctance of government to implement and sustain programs that work. The real mystery is that poor people who are eligible for these programs are denied access. The real mystery is the continuation of policies that perpetuate poverty and sabotage the economies of inner-city America.

In 1998, another commission came to the grim conclusion that America is moving backwards in its efforts to secure equity for minority citizens. This backward drift means that: (1) only one-third of new entrants into the labor force will be inner-city minorities; (2) many cities are becoming unproductive wastelands; (3) Black children are three times as likely as White children to grow up poor; (4) Black families are severely limited in income when compared to the typical White family; and (5) Black family unemployment is no longer static.

The United States government has dismantled entitlements, and the Church has to pick up the mantle based on its Biblical mission. "Go ye therefore, and teach all nations, baptizing them in the name of the Father, and of the Son, and of the Holy Ghost: Teaching them to observe all things whatsoever I have commanded you: and, lo, I am with you always, even unto the end of the world. Amen" (Matt. 28:19-20, KJV).

There was nothing more disturbing to Jesus in His own day than the inhumanity He witnessed in society. He was particularly appalled by the lack of compassion so evident in the religious communities of His time. He encountered an unsympathetic religious establishment, which demonstrated no concern for the suffering of the people around them. A religion is not worth following if it does not make you sensitive to the suffering of others, empathetic toward the less-fortunate, and actively compassionate toward all others, whatever their condition.

Jesus teaches us this during His visit to the pool of Bethesda, which was a type of nursing home or convalescent home located in the heart of the Jewish religious capital. During Jesus' visit to Jerusalem for the Jewish religious holidays, He visited the house of mercy with its five porches full of suffering people (see John 5:2-9). John indicates in his Gospel that there lay a great multitude of impotent people: blind, hurt, and withered. These individuals were the helpless who lacked the basic abilities to function in society. They had no skills, no education, and no hope. The blind could not see the area in which they lived. The ones with withered or deformed limbs found it impossible to secure gainful employment. Jesus came into this place, and it was just like Him to show that where hopelessness abounds helplessness also prevails. The Urban Church is in a similar situation today.

The Church must emphasize the following facts of community development: (1) a commitment to serving the poor and other needy members of humanity; (2) a keen sense of respect for the need of people and the impact of developments on a fragile ecology (3) a deep sense of responsibility to generate resources for the purpose of bringing balance between human needs and material good; (4) sense of calling for the Church to come of age; and (5) a desire to meet the real and true needs of the people the Church is called to serve.

The Church must bring to this equation a development enterprise, what can also be called the "prophetic imperative." The Church must find a way to contribute to the development of neighborhood economics and outreach ministries. The Church should recall the mission of prophetic witness by raising critical questions about the moral and social effects of market economics. This constitutes part of Dr. Martin Luther King, Jr.'s unfinished agenda. Perhaps Mahatma Gandhi best expressed the prophetic spirit of religion when he described the seven deadly sins as politics without principle, wealth without work, commerce without morality, pleasure without conscience, knowledge without character, science without humanity, and worship without sacrifice.

In Isaiah 61:1-4 and Luke 4:18-19, several key phrases effectively sum up the ministry of the Church. The Church has been divinely anointed to preach the Good News to the poor, bind up the brokenhearted, proclaim freedom to the captives, release prisoners from darkness, and proclaim the year of the Lord's favor. The Church is challenged to address the "spirit of despair" (Isa. 61:3, NIV). In Isaiah 61:4, the prophetic message states: "They will rebuild the ancient ruins and restore the places long devastated; they will renew the ruined cities that have been devastated for generations" (NIV). Who are "they"? Perkins claims that "they" are the inhabitants of the ruined and devastated places who have received the good news of the gospel."[1] In other words, the mission of the Messiah is our mission: empowering those living in the ruined cities of America.

Interestingly, the word Jesus uses for the intended recipients of His Gospel (see Matt. 28:19) is the Greek phrase *ta ethne*, from which we get the English word "ethnic." Jesus tells His disciples to teach and make disciples and for those new disciples, in turn, to be empowered to go and make other disciples.[2] We must recognize that an isolated call to serve the poor is not the call that God gives us. Rather, God's call comes in the form of a call to serve in the context of a particular parish or community of faith. Dietrich Bonhoeffer was a Lutheran pastor in Nazi Germany. In his book, *The Cost of Discipleship*, he explains the soul searching he went through in deciding to return to Germany in 1939 to face certain suffering. He writes, "The road to faith passes through obedience to the call of Jesus. Unless a definite step is demanded, the call vanishes into thin air, and if men imagine that they can follow Jesus without taking this step, they are deluding themselves like fanatics."[3] That is where we are in the Church—called to demonstrate our faith through obedience to Christ.

The Church of Jesus Christ is no stranger to the hopelessness of the inner city. Bill Pannell says:

> The Bible does not simply convey the story of a rural and pastoral life for God's people. Human beings may have begun in a garden, but human history began in a city.... The culmination of history is the descent of the city of God from heaven.... A prophet may be recruited while plowing, but he most certainly will deliver his message in the capital city. That's where the buttons, the levers, and the strings are that control the destinies of people in rural parts.[4]

The ministry of churches in the city is full of challenges, and it is in the midst of those challenges that we sometimes feel the greatest resistance. When we are faced with the challenge of being effective leaders in our communities, it is comforting to feel God's presence and to know that His glory surrounds us.

While leading the children of Israel through the wilderness, Moses sought the presence of God's glory as a sign of God's favor. God placed Moses in a cleft in the rock and covered Moses with His hand until He passed by (see Exod. 33:23). Consequently, Moses was protected from the face of God, yet privileged to see the glory of God. As we face the challenges in our cities, we do not see the face of God. But we do see His glory. As His glory comes, it requires us to sacrifice our ambition, popularity, and status.

The cry of God through Moses, in Exodus 8:20, to "let my people go" is still meaningful in our urban communities today. Yet how can the people be set free if we who are called to free them are not yet free? The Pharaoh of this day is not embodied in one man but is generally manifested as the spirit of pervasive and menacing evil. Furthermore, it seems that the religious community of this age has embraced this evil spirit and too easily cohabitates with it. The righteous and unrighteous seem to be equally afflicted with the plagues of our modern-day bondage. In Exodus 7–11, God inflicted Pharaoh with ten plagues: water flowing as blood, frogs, gnats, flies, diseased livestock, boils and sores on people and animals, thunder and hail, locusts, darkness, and the death of the firstborn in each Egyptian family. Yet, God protected the Hebrews from each plague. Today, our plagues include crime, drug abuse, incurable sexually transmitted diseases, political upheaval, broken families, weak moral values, teen pregnancy, school dropouts, depression, and unemployment. Our enemies use every philosophy and fleeting doctrine to challenge our Christian values (see Eph. 4:14; Col. 2:8). Have we so embraced the norms of corporate competitiveness that God has allowed Satan to unleash these plagues upon us? Is God demonstrating His disapproval because we have failed to heed His call?

God afflicted Pharaoh because he failed to recognize God's sovereign rule. The Church in urban America is plagued and sorely needs to allow God's righteousness to direct our ministries so that we may experience His deliverance and liberation. When the Church experiences liberation, community economic development is born. "Let my people go" is still meaningful (Exod. 8:20, NIV). Today's urban ministries, however, must be unceasingly creative and entrepreneurial in order to face a more complicated form of evil.

The Church in the 21st century must focus on the needs of the whole community of faith, as well as the local communities in which we are situated. The message of the Church must address the physical and spiritual needs not only in faith but also in deeds. The Bible speaks about Jesus doing good deeds, which means He had an active concern for the welfare of other people. That concern took on many different forms because there were different needs to be met. Jesus fed those who were hungry. He gave sight to the blind. He strengthened the lame so that they could walk again. He comforted the sick and the bereaved. He cast out the devils of those who were mentally disturbed. All of these were survival needs. In the ministry of Jesus, however, they were part and parcel of His spiritual mission to prepare His followers for a place with Him in heaven. "He opened his mouth, and taught them" (Matt. 5:2, KJV), and He knew then what every effective pastor knows today—saving souls should be our priority in this world.

Such a broad-based approach to the business of the Church is particularly redemptive and progressive for urban Americans who still struggle under an enormous burden of stress and instability. Religion has always been civilization's most reliable answer to the trauma of change. Because religion is anchored in "that which changeth not" and "that which is the same yesterday, today, and forever," the Church is perceived by the community to be built on the Rock of stability—Jesus Christ—that transcends change. However, to sustain its effectiveness, the Church must always be alert to new areas of ministry that constant change may produce. The mission, that is to say, the business of the Church, remains or ought to remain the same. But the responsible Church, as a community of believers in a changing world, has no mission if it does not resonate with the realities of the lives and circumstances of the people it exists to serve. There is no need to relate here the litany of evils the Urban Church is now called to address. However, to present a few of these offers some perspective on the task we face: children having children, welfare reform, the enormously disproportionate incarceration of Black youths, homelessness, the scourge of crack cocaine and other dangerous habit-forming drugs, AIDS, and unemployment. Each of these conditions is a disguise, a mask, that hides the suffering of the individual case. Oftentimes, that suffering is so overwhelming it smothers the spirit.

The Church must recognize that its spiritual business cannot always be separated from the maintenance of business. In dealing with the body and soul, the salvaging of one often requires the sacrificing of the other. This is good practical theology properly infused with the social consciousness of the Sermon on the Mount (see Matt. 5:3—7:27). It is a theology that demands empowerment, both spiritual and economic. There are five key elements to be recognized when we begin to address our theology of Christian community economic development:

- The Christian community economic development approach is mission-focused and rooted in Biblical principles.
- Economic empowerment is a reasonable response to the fact we are presently in the world but not of it. Being in the world requires the full armor of faith to survive.
- The Church's mission must recognize that the business of the Church cannot always be separated from the business of society, for men and women are both body and soul. In pursuit of the spiritual realm, the pastor who forgets or ignores the fact that his basic responsibilities must begin where the people are does so at his own peril and at the peril of his congregation.
- It is clear none of the freedoms we cherish can survive in the vacuum of economic deprivation. Thus, spiritual redemption begins with a full stomach, a warm place to sleep, education, and a hope for something more than perpetual handouts.
- The Church is the soul of America; if the Church is going to save souls, we must start in our neighborhoods, communities, and cities.

LET GOD DREAM ON YOU

The Book of Nehemiah is an excellent example of a biblical theology of community economic development. Nehemiah was a businessman, administrator, and a lay minister. He is certainly a model to be followed in a broken society if we wish to bring healing to a nation sick with sin and immorality. Nehemiah was a cupbearer for King Artaxerxes. When a group of Jews visited the capital of Persia, Nehemiah asked them how his people back home were doing. When Nehemiah heard of the plight of his people, he wept and mourned for days (see Nehemiah 1:4-11). But, there was no pity party; instead, he prayed to God. That is what Urban Church leaders must do: let God dream on them. From this metaphor, we can learn some principles for community economic development: (1) the importance of prayer; (2) the importance of a commitment to meet needs; (3) the principle of self-reliance; (4) the principle of cooperation; (5) the importance of recognizing the "God Factor"; (6) the importance of infrastructure; (7) the importance of seeking God's direction; and (8) the importance of spiritual entrepreneurship.

"In the beginning God created the heavens and the earth" (Gen. 1:1, NIV). "If anyone takes words away from this book of prophecy, God will take away from him his share in the tree of life" (Rev. 22:19, NIV). Thus, the Bible opens with the majestic story of God creating everything out of nothing and ends with a warning that humankind could lose its most precious gift—a share in the holy city. What happens between Genesis and Revelation? Between the Alpha and the Omega? Between the beginning and end of civilization? Nowhere does that drama unfold more clearly than in the cities of then and now.

The city is the stage upon which humankind, with all its flaws and fragility, grows and develops in the story we call life. The city is a mark of progress in mankind's journey toward civilization. But it can also mark the depth of mankind's backward slide into an uncivilized condition. The word "city" appears several hundred times in the Bible, with names of specific cities adding many more references. From the day Adam and Eve were cast out of the Garden of Eden, humankind has been building cities. From the day our earliest ancestors gathered together in their first cities, God has been involved in the life of those cities.

The most common first impression of the Bible's setting is pastoral: prophets wandering the deserts, shepherds on a hillside, or Jesus preaching from a mountaintop or walking on the sandy shore. Yet, the urban theme in the Bible is crucial to understand its message. The city is the major social context in which the theological events of the Biblical message transpire. Throughout history, the city is the well-spring of thoughts, ideas, actions, and interactions. It is the pulse of people throbbing in rhythm to their times. It is the collective voice of people crying out in prayer to the holy God of life or the wanton god of pleasure.

The first city mentioned in the Bible is Enoch (see Gen. 4:17). Its founding father was the murderer Cain, who was sent into exile by

God. Is Cain to be the prototype of all city builders? Are we to inter-pret the urban theme in the Bible as symbolic of human rebellion against God? A brief walk through the earliest cities introduced in Genesis would seem to confirm this concept. The second city men-tioned in the Bible has no name until God gives it one, symbolizing the action God took against the pride and arrogance of His people. He named the city Babel. What could be more symbolic of all that is wicked than the name of the third city, Sodom? We can walk beyond Genesis, through all the pages of the Old Testament, building a case for the inherent evil of cities. We can cry out with Micah against the city filled with violence, cheaters, and liars. We can echo the prophet Ezekiel by declaring, "The land is full of bloodshed and the city is full of injustice" (9:9, NIV). From the beginning of time, the city has been the setting for some of the most heinous crimes and the greatest depravity. It is the birthplace, homeland, and breeding ground of all that is evil in the eyes of righteous people, as well as the eternal Lord.

Why, then, should we be called to urban community economic development? Why should the Church not join those who have gathered their families and—along with any of the good, godly peo-ple still to be found—flee the city? Why not turn our backs on the shootings, the drug lords, the prostitution, extortion, injustice, and all of the indignities of the city? Thousands have already done so. Across our land, cities that were once thriving and alive have become virtual ghost towns. Business and commercial enterprises have fled to subur-bia. Why should we not follow their lead and escape while we still have time?

- Because the city, mostly out of economic necessity, is where most of the African-American people live.
- Because the city is where the power of God is needed most.
- Because the city is where we can make the greatest impact on the largest number of people with the greatest areas of need.
- Because the Bible gives us a clear, undebatable mandate to carry out a responsible and effective urban ministry.

Should the Church take up this task alone without divine guidance? No. Standing in sharp contrast to the Biblical examples of evil cities are the cities built by God's own direction. To these sheltering havens or, as Joshua described them, "[cities] of refuge" (Josh. 21:13, KJV), oppressed people, often wrongly accused of a crime, could flee and hide until a fair trial could be arranged. These cities were symbols of mercy and justice. They were built by divine plan, not human pride. Transforming our own declining cities into neighborhoods of acceptance and achievement is the very impetus for urban ministry. The "Promised Land" is the fulfilled promise of urban life.

Although the prophets of old were deeply aware of the potential for evil to germinate in the city, they were equally aware of its potential for good. Even when Ezekiel condemned the city, he ended his writings with a description of the restored city whose very name symbolized the presence of God. Isaiah, too, longed for restoration of the people who made up his city. He concluded his prophecy by reaching for the highest name possible by which to call the restored people. "They shall call thee, The city of the LORD, The Zion of the Holy One of Israel" (Isa. 60:14, KJV). We, too, can accomplish the same by a creative initiative in the area of business. When Jesus inaugurated His early ministry in Luke 4:18-19, He quoted from Isaiah 61. Jesus defined His life by preaching the Good News to the poor, the prisoners, the blind, and the oppressed. This is community economic development from the bottom up. As Pannell states:

> In a world where misery is the prevailing reality—especially among urban populations—our task is clear: to ask the Bible to speak to us from a vantage below, from the bottom up. We must recover a biblical view of salvation from the bottom up rather than from the top down, as is now the prevailing model. The task should not be all that difficult. The Bible was written in many situations of misery, deprivation and need.[5]

The basis of the call to community economic development as a part of the outreach mission is found not in the Great Commission but in the Great Commandment.

Here then are two instructions of Jesus—a great commandment: "love your neighbor," and a great commission: "go and make disciples." What is the relation between the two? Some of us behave as if we thought them identical. So that if we share the gospel with somebody, we consider we have completed our responsibility to love him. But no...God created man, who is my neighbor, a body-soul-in-community. Therefore, if we love our neighbor as God made him, we must inevitably be concerned for his total welfare, the good of his soul, his body, and community.[6]

Community economic development brings us face-to-face with the physical as well as spiritual needs of the people. Effective social action involves a willingness to create resources to meet the people's need for food, clothing, housing, and education.

1 John M. Perkins, ed., *Restoring At-Risk Communities: Doing It Together and Doing It Right* (Grand Rapids: Baker Book House, 1996), 31.

2 Ibid, 39.

3 Dietrich Bonhoeffer, *The Cost of Discipleship* (New York: Macmillan Publishing Co., 1963), 78.

4 William Pannell, *Evangelism From the Bottom Up* (Grand Rapids: Zondervan Publishing House, 1992), 37.

5 Ibid, 37.

6 John R. Stott, *Christian Mission in the Modern World* (Downers Grove, IL: InterVarsity Press, 1975), 27.

Chapter 4

Funding an Underfunded Vision—The Need "For Profit" And "Not For Profit"

When we began Country Preacher Foods, Inc., its purpose was to provide financial support for the education of impoverished inner-city children through the sale of quality products. The mission statement of Country Preacher Foods, Inc. is as follows:

> Country Preacher Foods, Incorporated, will produce and sell high-quality cookies, chips, and meats to generate proceeds for college education tuition for at-risk inner-city youth. Country Preacher Foods, Inc. is dedicated to providing the disadvantaged and/or high-risk children of urban America with the leadership and financial resources to get the education they will need to rise above their current economic status, and to become successful and contributing members of society.

Fulfilling this mission is important because it allows us to sponsor and assist inner-city youth with the financial resources to obtain the college education they need to improve their economic status.

If students at the sixth-grade level with a "want-to" attitude could look beyond their present environment and know that, if they finish school with a 3.0 G.P.A. or better, they are guaranteed funds for a college education and a summer job during college. Then they would know that the odds are no longer against them. Thus, their opportunity is certain.

Chapter 5

WHY CHURCHES SHOULD BE INVOLVED IN BUSINESS

For urban churches, the most difficult part of getting into business is creating relationships with large companies, especially when those companies are not naturally motivated to do business with the Urban Church. Articulating a common ground that still respects differences requires intelligence and a larger vision on everyone's part. All parties must understand that "economics is at the heart of the way our system and country and state function. Any search for equality therefore must be wedded to the pursuit of sound economics in the relationship."[1] Extending the concept of "sound economics" to include the formation of strong communities might seem like a daunting task, but at Historic Little Rock Missionary Baptist Church and Country Preacher Foods, Inc. we have discovered that corporate America listens to that message and eagerly collaborates with its business strategy.

Whatever the differences in experiences, values, and expectations, the 21st-century Church's collaboration with business has to be nurtured if it is to expand opportunities for those at the bottom of the economic pyramid. If the mission of the Church is to be achieved, something new and creative has to happen to the opportunity schedule of those at the bottom. This can be a difficult issue, not only in the corporate world but in the Church as well. Successful people are often those with discipline, ambition, pride, and an achieving spirit. They are not beggars, so they wonder what their connection is to the poor. It is difficult for working people to understand why we need to pay attention to those who have fallen behind. Just as the Church must enlighten the spirit of corporate America as to its role in the community, so must parishioners open their hearts to their own less-fortunate brethren. The pastor is the individual to remind comfortable people of what Jesus said in Matthew 26: "The poor you will always have with you" (v. 11, NIV). We do not all get what we deserve in life. The uncomfortable fact is that most of what we have was not deserved at all but was an unearned social benefit. Those who missed out on such benefits are left behind. Part of the American psyche is built on the pretense that social structures do not matter; it is the individual struggle that counts. Out of this naïve view flow cruel attitudes declaring that the poor deserve their poverty. It is very difficult to stir comfortable people into action on behalf of the poor. In addition to all this, the government is controlled by the upper echelon of society—people who flatter themselves with the illusion that all of their achievements are the result of their own efforts.

It should be obvious to everyone by now that the political process will reflect such naïve beliefs; thus, entitlements and social programs will not be supported within such a set of beliefs. Politicians are often funded by elites. Therefore, we find ourselves living not in a democracy, but in a plutocracy—a society ruled by the wealthy. If free voices, such as pastors, allow themselves to be muted, movement toward real community becomes far less likely. This real community would thus occur—if at all—only incidentally once the powerful money forces have had their agendas satisfied. Living within a plutocracy can produce a litany of evils: pollution of the rivers in poor communities; movement of jobs out of America to countries that allow the exploitation of labor; false advertising; the sale of unsafe products and other forms of consumer fraud; corrupt influence over legislation that governs prices, profits, and taxes; and pervasive control of the media to, in turn, control the tastes, habits, appetites, and priorities of an unsuspecting public.

Given all the available Biblical scholarship, as well as a complete analysis of the history of Jesus, one is not likely to be confused about what a society would be like if it followed the model of Jesus. No one would be penalized on account of language, economic background, or social standing. It would be difficult to confuse how Jesus would feel about some people starving, while other people have so much they have to build bigger barns to hold their surplus. A simple student of the Bible could describe how He felt about the blind, the homeless, the beggars, the lame and palsied bodies, or abused women and children. As people representing God's kingdom, we should have little doubt about where the kingdom of God is calling us—to the creation of justice in the world by alleviating suffering. In our world, that means that we must acquire economic power.

The 21st-century pastor and Church have the moral obligation to help create businesses and provide jobs and social services for the poor. The development of a for-profit company is formulated out of the preceding ethos and experiences. What location is to real estate, negotiation is to the Church. To move properly into the often tricky nature of business, we must be cognizant of transforming the win-lose mentality of business into a win-win proposition by making a crucial point: profits often reflect values such as hard work, good organization, and individual effort, but they can be put in the service of the world beyond the individual. On a very basic level, the use of profit preserves the practical efficiencies of capitalism, but it puts it into the service of the community. In a subtle fashion, this strategy reconnects individual and community interests.

The key to the successes of the Historic Little Rock Missionary Baptist Church and Country Preacher Foods, Inc., even with little and sometimes no capital, was to negotiate a market for a company that had not been successfully reaching the people in the inner city. For example, a company named Bettermade Potato Chips had the number one potato chip in the state of Michigan, but not in Detroit, and Detroit alone contained one million consumers. Bettermade was happy but not satisfied. This situation gave Country Preacher Foods Inc. room to negotiate. We asked the manager/owner of Bettermade, "Are you interested in selling potato chips or bags that have the name 'Bettermade'?"

His answer was clear, "We're interested in selling potato chips."

Our response to Bettermade was specific. "If that's the case, would you mind a private labeling for Country Preacher for the inner-city consumer market that has eluded you?"

"It's a deal," he said.

We began to ask for help from radio disc jockeys, Black newspapers, and the Black Chamber of Commerce. They were more than happy to assist us because of their community pride and the intrinsic value of the cause. The jobs we need in America require a marketplace in our community, which means we must work with and through other people.[2] The strategy of the Urban Church must include a commitment to our own community that is demonstrated by an ability to create alliances with communities outside of our own.

You probably would be surprised to know that there are institutions (schools, hospitals, prisons, etc.) that are waiting for someone like you or your organization to bring forth a creative concept. It is vital that we realize that corporate America is more than willing to do business with the Urban Church, assuming both parties can find mutual ground and mutual economic respect. The margin of profit may be small, but if one can demonstrate growth in profits, however small they may be, the Urban Church has a chance to develop a relationship with the business world.

Michael Novak wrote in his insightful book, *Business as a Calling: Work and the Examined Life,* "Business is about creating goods and services, jobs and benefits and new wealth that didn't exist before. The nature of business is creative and can transform the conditions of human life for the better or the worse."[3] There is a way for big business to give back to the community. Entrepreneurs have a special role to play in bringing hope and economic progress to communities of faith that cannot support their outreach ministries. Business can be seen as the best hope of impoverished outreach programs. One of the noblest callings inherent in all of business is to raise the standard of living in the community it serves. If the Church is to lift urban communities out of poverty, then the Church needs those of us with ideas and capital to invest. We can create the industries, jobs, and wealth that will be a base upon which to build stable communities that foster the sort of commitment shown to us by Christ's example. To that end, engaging in business and creating new wealth is every church's moral assignment and is especially imperative in the 21st century. In a capitalist society, entrepreneurship is a sure road to opportunity for outreach ministries.

The Urban Church's spiritual value system often views life in a circular, holistic fashion. The ancestors of African Americans passed on the belief that they were not merely human beings having a spiritual experience but spiritual beings having a human experience. Spiritual life arises out of a life lived, and simultaneously, a lived life is a manifestation of the Spirit. Separating the two only harms us. Arguably, economic life offers an arena where one can begin to reconnect the two. The 21st-century Church must once again become one with the poor, as well as one with the community. Not long ago, one could claim with relative confidence that there was no gap between the Church and community; they were one. Today, however, the link between the Church and the community is now probably more myth than reality. The gap between them is getting wider. The Urban Church is often separate from the community in part because the community has become capitalist whereas the Urban Church has not.

Whether it began as James H. Cone and Gayraud J. Wilmore say with "urban migration"[4] or with what C. Eric Lincoln and Lawrence H. Mamiya call the "saved cosmos,"[5] the schism exists. There is no dichotomy between sacred and secular or what Lincoln and Mamiya call "partial differentiation"[6] where power and influence diminish. The consequence of all this, as we move further in the 21st century, is a severe crisis in supportive services for the Urban Church. Even though it is disheartening to hear, we can no longer assume the younger generation will have any affinity for the Church and its work.

The ultimate challenge for the Urban Church is to express its mission by empowering the people it serves, not only to learn theology but to practice what you have learned from theology from the grassroots up. The gap must be closed between socioeconomic classes, and we must generate the wealth to deliver a generation. The 21st-century Church must become the liberating agent that reintegrates the sacred and the secular.

There should be no doubt in anyone's mind about the critical role the Church will play in the survival of our urban communities. As we move further into the 21st century, the Church will share an even greater burden to enhance the well-being of our ministries. If the Church assumes this burden, it makes sense to understand its own strengths and weaknesses. Consequently, a thorough analysis of the building of economic power through the rapid formation of business enterprises should begin with the current businesses within the United States. Those businesses are more likely to be sympathetic to the plight of our urban communities. After we have documented where we are and where we would like to be, we can begin to construct a workable strategy for focusing our resources intelligently to accomplish the economic goals of which we speak.

Although we have seen growth in urban businesses, the depth and breadth of these new ventures tend to be limited by under-capitalization, marketing obstacles, and a host of other problems that include prevailing tax policies in urban areas. These businesses emerge in a difficult climate, and their continued existence signals a belief in economic inventiveness. For example, 94 percent of all African-American businesses are sole proprietorships, which are good for the individual but does not provide much leverage for the community where the business is located. According to a survey by the Commerce Department's Census Bureau, the number of African-American businesses in the United States has increased from 362,000 in 1992 to 500,000 in 1997. This equates to a 38 percent increase during a five-year period.

Not only was the number of African-American businesses increasing, so was the total number of companies. The number of all United States companies rose 14 percent, from 12 million to 13.7 million during the same five-year time period. The 500,000 African-American businesses constitute 3.1 percent of the total United States business base. Concurrently, these 500,000 businesses generated $20 billion in annual revenue, which comprises just under 1 percent of the nation's total receipts. Approximately 54 percent of all Black companies had receipts under $10,000; fewer than 2,000 had sales of $1,000,000 or more. The 189 African-American owned companies with 100 or more employees accounted for $2 billion in gross receipts or about 14 percent of the total receipts for all African-American firms. These figures reveal that African-American businesses are disproportionately small.

The African-American businesses with the largest dollar volume of receipts in 1987 were automotive dealers and service stations. Business services formed the second-largest industry group in terms of dollar volume receipts generated by Black-owned businesses.

The ten top metropolitan areas with the largest number of African-American-owned firms accounted for 36 percent of the national total for African-American-owned businesses and 36 percent of gross receipts. It is interesting to note that of the top ten areas, seven or eight have African-American majorities or a sizable African-American minority. Currently, African Americans constitute 12.1 percent of the United States population. We would expect a similar proportion of businesses to be African-American. Thus the Urban Church could play a role in that activity. Of course the Church's business role is primarily suited to another context—the extension of its mission into the community. However, many urban churches struggle to extend themselves into the community, not because they do not have the desire but due to a lack of funding.

GOOD BUSINESS IS WIN-WIN

For urban churches, the most difficult task is making the transition out of the sanctuary and into the board room. An important component of this shift is to create relationships with large companies by motivating them to do business with the Urban Church. As stated by Perkins, "...economics is at the heart of the way our system and state and country function." Any desire on the part of the Urban Church to sit with confidence in the boardrooms of America's corporations must be connected to the pursuit of sound economics in the relationship. Outlined below are a few examples of strategies the Historic Little Rock Missionary Baptist Church has successfully implemented.

FARMER JACK GROCERY STORES

At one time, Farmer Jack Grocery Stores had more than one hundred stores in the state of Michigan and twenty-two stores in the city of Detroit. It was, by far, the largest grocery chain in Detroit. Therefore, it was an obvious target for Country Preacher Foods, Inc. We sent a letter to the CEO of Farmer Jack outlining the mission and purpose of Country Preacher Foods and requesting an opportunity for a partnership. Approximately a week after we sent the letter, we called and requested a meeting with the CEO. He granted our request. Also representing Farmer Jack at the meeting were the marketing director, the vice president, and the snack department manager.

The Country Preacher Foods presentation focused on three key issues: (1) the mission of the Country Preacher Foods, Inc. was to generate income and revenue to help the youth who graduated from Detroit's high schools obtain funding for college; (2) the purpose of the meeting was to develop a relationship with Farmer Jack Grocery Stores and request that Farmer Jack give something back to the community by waiving the usual store shelf slotting fee and aiding in the marketing of our cookies and meats; and (3) the larger strategy for a for-profit business partnering with a non-profit company was simple: respecting both the efficiencies and utilities of sound business practices, while simultaneously tying the business to a larger social good—the education of promising African-American students.

The CEO of Farmer Jack listened with intensity and emotion. He came to the conclusion he would recommend our products for placement in all twenty-two Detroit stores for a pilot project. One of the reasons he gave was that the church had a relationship with the Detroit Black media. Thus, we could generate customers for Farmer Jack Stores. The pending relationship would serve both Farmer Jack and Country Preacher Foods because it made good business sense. The Farmer Jack Company would get new customers from our network of churches, civic, and community groups, and our products would be sold in one of the largest markets in the city.

At the end of the negotiations, the CEO of Farmer Jack stated his staff would work with Country Preacher Foods in every way to make this collaboration a success. The twenty-two stores placed our products on their shelves, charged no slotting fees, and with well-defined and significant advertising and promotion, the Farmer Jack/Country Preacher Foods partnership experienced great success.

MEIJER SUPERSTORES

Meijer Superstores are the largest of their kind in Michigan, and they are still growing. Meijer is not just a food store, but a one-stop superstore that sells thousands of items used by consumers on a daily basis. Although headquartered in Grand Rapids, Michigan, Meijer has stores located throughout the United States. Country Preacher Foods sent a letter to Mr. Fred Meijer, CEO of Meijer, Incorporated. Our research indicated that Mr. Meijer was a Christian and was community-oriented. In fact, one of his personal heroes was Frederick Douglass. Although the request in the original letter to Mr. Meijer was similar to the one to Farmer Jack, there was a slight difference. Where the main contact with Farmer Jack was an employee of the company, Mr. Meijer was the actual owner of the Meijer Superstores, so our approach was more direct with him. The Country Preacher Foods introductory letter focused on what is happening in the inner city and how corporate America must respond with opportunities, not handouts. We shared our belief that institutions within the Black community must be in a position to change the economic conditions for their constituents. Our correspondence evidently touched Mr. Meijer's heart because he set up a meeting with us at his Grand Rapids headquarters. The fifteen Meijer participants at the meeting included people from the division of marketing, advertising, snacks and meats, and art and design. This might have seemed intimidating, but it showed his commitment to our mission. Our presentation to the Meijer Company lasted about thirty-five minutes with an additional twenty minutes for questions and answers. We discussed the Country Preacher Foods manufacturing division, the pricing for the products, and the number of stores to be recommended for the pilot project.

The recommendation was to put our cookies in 121 stores and our meats in 5 stores in metropolitan areas. Mr. Meijer said to his managers, "I want this to work." The meats did well during the pilot, but the cookies in the outlying areas sold poorly. The reason was because our networking and marketing opportunities were limited to the urban community and were not as effective in rural areas. Eventually, the cookie order for the project was revamped to concentrate on the metropolitan areas along with the meats.

ALLIANT KRAFT FOOD COMPANY

We met with the CEO of the area division of Alliant Kraft Food Company and requested that Country Preachers Foods products be marketed to the hospitals in which Alliant serves a substantial market. The Country Preacher staff was given forty-five minutes to make the presentation. The meeting began informally and moved into a discussion of the mutual business benefits of a partnership between the two companies. Alliant Kraft Food recognized that Country

Preacher cookies would complement their food offerings in hospital facilities. They also decided to consider our meats. The cookies would be used for lunches in the hospitals, and the meats would be distributed to other institutions served by Alliant Foods. Alliant Foods realized those who benefit from the community have an obligation to give something back to their community. The vision of returning value to the community is one African Americans must suggest that corporate CEOs consider.

However, Alliant Kraft still wondered what was in it for them. We answered by saying that Alliant Kraft and Country Preacher Foods could work on government bids and contracts that require minority vendor participation. This could be the beginning of a relationship built on reciprocity, not generosity.

STATE OF MICHIGAN CORRECTIONS DEPARTMENT

Another major example of Country Preacher Foods marketing and distribution efforts involved the Corrections Department of the State of Michigan. The state prisons house several thousand young African-American males and females, which was a great reason for our business proposal. The reality is that everyone is doing business with the state prison system except Black businesses, even though 67 percent of the prison population is African-American.

We made an appointment with the director of the State Corrections System, requesting a pilot program in ten prisons with the chance to expand if the product sold well. We subsequently had meetings with officials from each individual prison, which had a committee that included prisoners themselves. Country Preacher Foods discussed the following: (1) proceeds would go to education in the inner city (the committees responded favorably to this because educational opportunities reduce the possibilities of going to prison); (2) all people perform better if they have purpose and a mission; (3) the worth of African Americans in general needs to be asserted; and (4) in addition to all of the social reasons to support Country Preacher Foods, the company also produces an excellent product.

The prisoners we worked with were very loyal and always seemed to make an effort to send the message of Country Preacher Foods back to the community. There is now 100 percent cooperation between the company and the prisoners, and the work of the prisoners has been superb.

BE STRONG AND COURAGEOUS

I must admit that not all of our corporate experiences have been productive. Some of the experiences reflect the heritage of major corporations using their profits for their own purposes. This was made clear when I approached Gordon Foods, one of the largest food distributors in Michigan. The company's lobby is filled with biblical quotations, and the overall image of the company attempted to project Christian values. It seemed like we could have a mutually beneficial relationship. I asked Gordon Foods to include just one of our products with the more than 7,500 they distribute. The response of Gordon Foods revealed how much still needs to be changed in the corporate climate of White America. The Gordon Foods executive told me, "I'm not in business to put you in business. I have foundations to take care of people like you." He then offered to write a $10,000 check. Neither I nor the rest of the Country Preacher Foods staff wanted charity; our mission was to establish *bona fide* business relationships. Therefore, we declined the offer.

We must all remember no matter how sound the business proposal or how beneficial the relationship will be to the urban community, there are companies who will say no. It is during these times we must be strong and courageous and continue to pursue with all diligence the growth of businesses in urban communities. We can change the hearts of corporations more easily by providing a clear rationale for the business relationship, being gracious, and never giving up hope.

It is important to include at this point what would be designated as "internal success actualization": a situation in which the would-be entrepreneur has completed the necessary steps to prepare for the rigors of the various business endeavors. You have to be strong if you are to have any chance of making this business journey successfully.

The pyramid of internal success requirements includes the following:

SPIRITUAL FORTITUDE • PHYSICAL FORTITUDE

INTELLECTUAL FORTITUDE • MAINTAIN MOTIVATION • PRESENTATION

MINIMIZE COSTS • FINANCIAL PREPARATION PURPOSE • UNDERSTANDING THE "WHY"

FAITH • SUPPORT BASE • MANAGE DEBT • HAVE A SPECIALTY

This is a pyramid of elements that will serve those at the base of America's economic pyramid.

1 John Perkins, *A Quiet Revolution: The Christian Response to Human Need, a Strategy for Today* (Pasadena, CA: Urban Family Publications, 1996), 138.

2 George K., Makechnie, *Howard Thurman: His Enduring Dream.* (Boston: Boston University Press, 1988), page 51.

3 Quoted in George C. Fraser, *Race for Success: The Ten Best Business Opportunities for Blacks in America* (New York: William Morrow and Co., 1998), 17.

4 Gayraud S. Wilmore and James H. Cone, eds., *Black Theology: A Documentary History* (Maryknoll, NY: Orbis Books, 1979),135.

5 C. Eric Lincoln and Lawrence H. Mamiya, *The Black Church in the African American Experience* (Durham, NC: Duke University Press, 1990), 135.

6 Ibid, 135.

Chapter 6

CLOSING—TAKING THE WORD INTO THE WORLD

The decline of our cities and the competition for dollars has brought the Urban Church to a crossroads where it must ask itself about its role in the world. In many poor neighborhoods, the economy revolves around diminishing welfare benefits and growing drug markets that have created a subculture of permanent dependency and violence. Compounding this scenario, government welfare programs have subtly enabled the development of the single-parent household as the norm for the family. Add to that picture an inept and ineffective big city educational system, and the results for inner-city residents have been predictably devastating. This condition compels us to bring the Word into the world through new strategies.

The ministry of Jesus reveals to us a Person who was concerned not only about making disciples but also making them whole human beings. When people were suffering, Jesus made them whole. This is also the responsibility of the Church in the community. This concept of wholeness can be articulated in several ways. Howard Thurman's "actualizing potential" and the idea of Nihilism as articulated by Cornel West frame the discussion of this responsibility. Thurman contends, "we live in a constant attempt to realize our potential, striving towards wholeness."[1] He continues, "The degree to which the potential in any expression of life is actualized marks the extent to which such an expression of life experiences wholeness, integration, community."[2]

West turns from the individual to a more abstract explanation when he asserts the following: "Nihilism is to be understood here not as a philosophic doctrine that there are no rational grounds for legitimate standards or authority; it is, far more, the lived experience of coping with a life of horrifying meaninglessness, hopelessness, and (most important) lovelessness."[3] West provides us with a fundamental understanding of the work of the Church. If we recognize both the realities stated by Thurman and the ideas outlined by West, we are faced with a different question: How do you get from the point of merely coping with meaningless, hopelessness, and lovelessness to the point of actualizing the Church's potential? Thurman and others wrestled with the question at a time when the threat of Nihilism—a philosophy that claims the world is without meaning, purpose, truth, or value—was not as prevalent as it is today. The Church's approach to wholeness (outreach) from the standpoint of meeting individuals where they are leads to bringing resources into use for outreach programs, which create a life of meaning, hope, and love. The task is immense, but it creates a set of specific attitudes and skills for those who accept the call.

WHAT IT TAKES TO BE A CHRISTIAN ENTREPRENEUR

Be warned. The path to entrepreneurship is not an easy road. What does it take to start your business as a Christian entrepreneur?

1. A "junkyard dog" determination. If you do not know what this means, you have never climbed a junkyard fence and encountered a guard dog trained to not let go of any intruder. True entrepreneurs do not let go! If one venture fails, then try another. If one product does not sell, then look for another idea. Just like the junkyard dog, hang on no matter what and stay focused.

2. A willingness to take a leap of faith. Successful entrepreneurs are not afraid to act on faith alone, but they have the God-given sense to plan thoroughly first.

3. An ability to focus on solutions, not on blame. Entrepreneurs are natural problem solvers. While everyone else is pointing and blaming, they are engaged in finding solutions and seeing new opportunities.

4. A high level of energy. A real entrepreneur never has a settling spirit. They never know when they are going to make the big sale. The people who are involved with them must also have a singular vision, enormous vitality, and constant anticipation.

5. A non-apologetic attitude about making money. Many church leaders seem to be ashamed to talk about money or to be accused of making money. Christian entrepreneurs cannot shy away from money if they want to provide for their communities.

6. A talent for recognizing their own assets and liabilities. They are able to find and utilize the talents of others. They believe they have the ability to do one or many things well but not the skills to do everything well. They learn to delegate.

7. An intelligent flexibility. Entrepreneurs are focused on the profit potential, not on the ingredients or chemical composition of the product.

8. A confident courage. Of all the qualities typically cited as crucial to the make up of a successful Christian entrepreneur, none is taken more for granted than pure courage. The entrepreneur is not afraid to take his/her presentation to the top decision makers of companies.

9. A strong faith. Christian entrepreneurs are always, of course, people of God and faithful to the cause.

10. Personal sacrifice. Christian entrepreneurs realize that personal sacrifices are inevitable. If customers see you face your responsibilities on behalf of the hopeless, loveless, and meaningless, you will be more likely to walk away with a deal.

A church must consider many things when preparing to serve through entrepreneurial activity. The goals, direction, and organization of the church are extremely important. When these key objectives are determined, a church can then move on to the next stages more easily. The ultimate goal of any church is to strengthen its fellowship and satisfy its many needs. According to James H. Cone, "Theology and ministry need to work together in order to bring bound people freedom."[4] Cone understands well the responsibility of the Church to continue its ministry and meet the needs of the community.

There are two obvious approaches when developing a business to generate resources for outreach ministries: the old-fashioned way and the "new-faith" way. Both require strategic planning. Although enthusiasm and reputation may be enough to convince church members, those traits will not hold much sway with bankers and other outside investors. When you are an urban church attempting to do business with a local bank, no amount of charm is going to convince them to open up their vaults for you. They want a business plan that tells your story. Sophisticated bankers will see right through any smoke screen. No matter which route you choose, your plan should follow the examples outlined in the previous chapters of this book.

Traditional divisions between religious communities and the business world have typically been mediated by government programs. However, these training, education, and entitlement programs have withered in the midst of a culture that overvalues the myth of the individual—a myth that refuses to recognize we are all part of a larger community. Whatever the changes, the needs of the poor remain: the hungry need food, the homeless need shelter, and the young need education. What shall we do when our culture turns its back on such needs?

For Christians, the answer lies in a return to our roots. For the Urban Church, those roots include a deeply entrenched understanding that the spiritual life enriches a life lived in the physical world, and the material realities of a life lived, in turn, reflect the spiritual bonds of the community. The tradition of the Urban Church should refuse an easy dualism between flesh and spirit or religion and community. We should expect our faith to have power.

Nowhere is this tradition more evident than in the quantity and quality of outreach ministries at the Historic Little Rock Missionary Baptist Church. Our faith and our ministries are the tools for putting our Christianity into practice. However, they are tools badly worn from overuse born of the withering of government support for the needy.

In this context, our church has decided to extend its presence into a part of the world where it is seldom found—the corporate world of profits and risks. If the world includes these activities, then the Church should be there as well. But the Church should be there in its traditional purpose of ministering to the needy. At Little Rock, we have also found a way to be in that world by pressing profit-making activities into the service of a non-profit foundation that serves the community. The realization of profit became socially motivated.

Revenues were an instrument for empowering our children and a means to speak to the business community. The growing success of that umbrella enterprise—Country Preacher Foods, Incorporated—illustrates how the practices of the world can make a place for the Word. The work of Christ in the city is essentially the sometimes complicated matter of redirecting business toward broader and more responsible solutions for the suffering around us.

1 Howard Thurman, *The Search for Common Ground: An Inquiry into the Basis of Man's Experience of Community* (Richmond, IN: Friends United Press, 1986), 87.

2 Ibid, 87.

3 Cornel West, *Prophesy Deliverance: An Afro-American Revolutionary Christianity* (Philadelphia: Westminster John Knox Press, 1982).

4 James H. Cone, "Black Theology in American Religion," *Journal of the American Academy of Religion 8* (1985): 197.

Appendix 1

------◆◆◆------

OUTREACH MINISTRIES SOLUTIONS

TABLE OF CONTENTS

INTRODUCTION

BIG PROBLEMS DEMAND BIG SOLUTIONS

As a poor Black child growing up in America, it was impossible for me to miss the pain and suffering of the people. There was a hopelessness associated with poverty. It was difficult to see, on one hand, the wealth of America so vividly portrayed on TV and, on the other hand, see a completely different world where no one worked and where government programs and crime were the only economic activity. It was a world of no jobs, no business opportunities, no new housing, no health care, no place for seniors, and no shoes for children in the winter. I did not like this world, and I vowed to help change it.

I was fortunate enough to have been raised in the Church, where I learned that through Jesus, all things are possible—including alleviating human suffering. God encourages us to dream big and trust Him. Giving yourself to God is akin to believing He will help you find the answers you need.

As a young preacher, I set out to make the world a better place for the glory of God. Through His will, I met Dr. Benjamin Hooks and was brought to Detroit. I found a city full of need but even more filled with opportunity. Detroit has a once-fabulous infrastructure and people unlike any other—people who love the Lord and never give up hope.

I found the best way to succeed in business is to surround yourself with people who also dream big and believe anything can be accomplished. There are enough obstacles to overcome in making a dream a reality without having the naysayers on your own team.

If there is one thread between all of our seemingly diverse business programs, it is to aim high, find those who share your dream and empower them to make it happen, and never give up. There is no way we could have ever built the businesses we have without our faith that God will provide.

LITTLE ROCK MISSIONARY BAPTIST CHURCH

THE PROBLEM

In May of 1973, 37 years after Little Rock Missionary Baptist Church was founded, the membership was down to less than fifty members. In addition, the congregation was divided about the dismissal of the previous pastor. Many more were not sure about the new, inexperienced twenty-nine-year-old preacher.

THE SOLUTION

In one of his sermons, Reverend Holley called all of the people to unite behind their love of Jesus and not fight over the scraps of the old church. Reverend Holley commissioned the congregation to build a better church, dedicated to serving the community as Jesus did. He spoke of Little Rock becoming an activist church where no social need would be rejected. He related his dream of a new church on Woodward Avenue where the congregation could bring all of their friends and family and unite to help each other in the love of God.

THE RESULT

In 1978, Little Rock Missionary Baptist Church moved to a historic church building. The church developed a mission of meeting the needs of the community and became involved in providing almost every social service. The membership of the church is now more than 3,000. The church has fostered more than a dozen successful businesses to support its programs.

Little Rock Missionary Baptist Church includes the following: 23 financially supported ministries, 3,000 K-12 students on 2 campuses, a homeless shelter, 147-bed senior care facility, a food service business, real estate developments, a family life center, health centers, 122 hospital beds, 62 full college scholarships per year, and more than 80 jobs created in Detroit.

SHOES FOR CHILDREN DRIVE

THE PROBLEM

As incredible as it seems, there are thousands of children in Detroit without shoes for the winter. This kind of poverty could not be ignored. When Rev. Holley became aware of this problem, he vowed Little Rock would do something about it.

THE SOLUTION

In 1985, Rev. Holley created the Shoes for Children Drive. It became a key outreach program for Little Rock. Rev. Holley and his congregation were able to raise enough money for the drive to buy more than 10,000 pairs of shoes and deliver them to poor children.

THE RESULT

The Shoes for Children Drive has given away more than 200,000 pairs of shoes to children in need. The drive is in its 20th year and gives away more than 20,000 shoes a year to qualified mothers at the State Fair Grounds. Every major shoe distributor has donated shoes and provided charitable pricing on others to further the impact of the drive.

COUNTRY PREACHER FOODS

THE PROBLEM

Dropping out of high school had become a big problem in the lives of many of our young people. They had no dream of going to college and joining the professional world. These young people did not think they could afford college. Rev. Holley told the students to remove the cost of college from their thinking and leave that problem to him and God.

THE SOLUTION

Rev. Holley created Country Preacher Foods in order to fund the scholarships he had promised. Mercy and goodness were promised in every bite. Every penny of profit goes to the scholarship fund. The recipes are based on treasured Southern recipes from Rev. Holley's grandmother. Cookies, potato chips, beverages, snack foods, and healthy, nutritional, and complete meals are now sold across America.

THE RESULT

Country Preacher Foods has diversified into the Food Service Company with a mission—educating young people. More than 60,000 meals a day are provided in Detroit Public Schools, the state prisons, and other institutional settings. A fleet of trucks make deliveries statewide. A complete product line continues to be sold at retail and wholesale markets. The profits from the food business allowed other church businesses to spin off and become reality.

CHIP FOUNDATION

THE PROBLEM

A college education was no longer attainable for many of the church and community's young people. This lack of hope for the future was dooming a generation. Rev. Holley felt that a church could not let one of its young people be denied a college education because of a lack of money.

THE SOLUTION

In 1990, Rev. Holley created the CHIP Foundation, which stands for Christians Helping in Partnership. CHIP is the fundraising and administrative component of the Scholarship Program. Students are assisted with identifying the right college, the scholarship process, and making accommodations for the financing of other expenses from the CHIP Grants.

THE RESULT

CHIP Scholars have attended more than 100 colleges and universities across the country. Every year the program has grown. It now has more than a dozen dedicated lines of financial support. Last year the CHIP Foundation funded 63 full scholarships. The whole outlook on college has changed among the young people because more and more students apply every year. Little Rock's goal is for every child in its membership to experience post-secondary education.

LITTLE ROCK NON-PROFIT HOUSING

THE PROBLEM

There was a shortage of safe new housing in the area around Little Rock. The housing stock was in great demand, which caused low-income people to overpay for their housing. The blight around the church was decreasing property values and killing economic development opportunities. The option of home ownership was out of reach for many people.

THE SOLUTION

Little Rock Housing was created to develop real estate in the community around the church. Creativity was used in locating and obtaining the properties, building and financing the units, and marketing the homes. Fifty-six new homes were built in Phase I. Little Rock Housing has a feeder system of buyers from the church congregation.

THE RESULT

All homes built have been sold and occupied. Phase II is now in the works with more than 200 homes planned. Little Rock Housing has future plans for condominiums, multi-unit and senior housing. The program has been a contributor to church programs by providing housing, jobs, and home ownership to members, while eliminating blight in the neighborhood.

COUNTRY PREACHER GAS STATION

THE PROBLEM

Most African Americans use gas stations, but almost no African Americans own gas stations. Gas stations in Detroit had become a symbol of the lack of economic opportunity. Little Rock decided to change this perception by opening and staffing a gas station and retail store.

THE SOLUTION

Country Preacher Gas Station opened as a BP station on Woodward Avenue near the church. The station employs people from Little Rock providing further economic benefit to the church membership. The station is being used as a training program to enable African Americans to enter the oil business.

THE RESULT

The station has been well supported by the community. Currently, eleven people work at the gas station full time. The station is earning more than $2 million per year. There are plans to further the station into a chain of stations, all providing community jobs, vital services, and support of the scholarship program.

DETROIT ACADEMY OF ARTS AND SCIENCES

THE PROBLEM

Detroit public schools had become dangerous, underachieving institutions that had failed our children. The dropout rate was 75 percent. Students could not read near their grade level and only 13 percent went on to college. Budget cuts and financial problems within the schools threatened to make the situation worse.

THE SOLUTION

Rev. Holley started the Detroit Academy of Arts and Sciences. The program has two campuses and plans for a third. The students wear uniforms and learn through a vigorous curriculum that prepares the students for real-world careers. Every child who graduates from the Academy is expected to attend college. Parents are involved in their child's education at every step of the way.

THE RESULT

DAAS has become the largest charter school in Michigan with more than 3,000 students. Every teacher at the Academy is certified. The promise of college financial aid has been extended to every DAAS student. It is essential that the scholarship fund grow because the need for it is growing exponentially. Rev. Holley views this as a good problem to have. DAAS students have received numerous scholarships and grants from hundreds of other scholarships.

COUNTRY PREACHER PHARMACY AND MEDICAL CENTER

THE PROBLEM

There was a need for a community pharmacy and medical center in the neighborhood around the church. Health care is a major problem with the poor. The lack of convenient facilities and the method of paying for it was contributing to an underserved, and therefore, unhealthy population.

THE SOLUTION

The Country Preacher Pharmacy and Medical Center opened on Woodward Avenue in October of 2006. This full-service pharmacy provides discount medications as well as dispenses health education materials and support. The Medical Center has plans to offer low cost in-the-field medical services as well.

THE RESULT

The Country Preacher Pharmacy and Medical Center is planning a state-of-the-art community health improvement program. The Center will be working with the Detroit Hope Hospital as an outreach center for the program. The additional healthcare services in the community will improve the quality of life for all.

O'DELL JONES NURSING HOME

THE PROBLEM

Growing old is a major problem for low-income people. In many cases, the elderly have been warehoused in facilities that are lacking in both dignity and amenities. Rev. Holley is committed to the concept of honoring our seniors by providing a loving and high-quality end-of-life option.

THE SOLUTION

The O'Dell Jones Nursing Home opened with 147 beds taking care of our seniors. These patients are treated as we would treat our own parents. A church committee works with the center to continue providing an ever-improving quality of life in the facility.

THE RESULT

Members of Little Rock and the community have the option of a loving place that will ensure their parents and grandparents are well taken care of in their final days. The facility provides more than 100 jobs and is one of the church's favorite missions. The goal of bringing dignity to our loved ones' final days is universally supported.

FAMILY LIFE CENTER

THE PROBLEM

Recreational opportunities in the community were going to vanish with the closure of the City of Detroit's Considine Recreation Center. A facility that had 70,000 feet of classrooms, a swimming pool, and three gyms was going to be shuttered, along with all the good the center accomplished.

THE SOLUTION

Little Rock Missionary Baptist Church took over the operation of the facility. A major overhaul of the facility converted the center to a state-of-the-art Family Life Center to further the programs of the church, which is located next door, and other community offerings.

THE RESULT

The recreation center was saved from closure. More than 40 programs now operate out of the Family Life Center with more planned. Forty employees have been able to keep their jobs. And instead of contracting and cutting back, the center has ambitious plans for the first time in generations.

ROCK PLAZA STRIP MALL

THE PROBLEM

There was a lack of viable retail services in the church community. There was also a corresponding lack of jobs and business ownership activity. A shopping plaza in the community was needed to end this dim situation and provide positive economic activity.

THE SOLUTION

The Rock Plaza Strip Mall was created on Woodward Avenue, just north of the church. The mall has 5 retail tenants, including a Subway Sandwich Shop owned by church members. The strip mall has encouraged other nearby economic activity, improving business and property values for all.

THE RESULT

The Rock Plaza Strip Mall has been open for four years and is fully leased. The success of the strip mall has led to the planning and opening of several other commercial retail developments.

DETROIT HOPE HOSPITAL

THE PROBLEM

Statistics show that Detroiters die a decade sooner than residents of Oakland County. We live to an average age of 64. In Oakland County, the average life span is 74. The poverty in Detroit is killing people before their time by denying them preventative medicine. The high number of uninsured and under-insured patients, as well as reduced access to health care, cause tremendous suffering in the city. In Detroit, despite the needs, clinics and hospitals have been closing or moving to the suburbs.

THE SOLUTION

Detroit Hope Hospital was created to take the health care to the public. A citywide health screening program was created and executed in partnership with Detroit churches and mosques. The mayor was recruited to be the public face for the Hope for Health Drive. Pharmaceutical companies would be partners in the screening programs as well as providing their drugs at a discounted rate.

THE RESULT

Detroit Hope Hospital is now open, providing services to the community. More than 300 jobs have been created, and a $5 million economic impact is projected for the hospital's first year. More than 200 churches are participating in the Hope for Health Drive. A tele-medicine program is in development to do additional community health screening. A television, radio, and print campaign is in development with the mayor as the spokesperson.

MIDDLE COLLEGE ACADEMY

THE PROBLEM

There are more than 50,000 young people from the ages of 17-19 in Detroit who have dropped out of high school. Essentially, they have dropped out of life, working in underpaying jobs or having no jobs at all. These students have given up on the dream of a better future. Many of these young people are filled with anger at their prospects.

THE SOLUTION

Rev. Holley created the Middle College Academy to give a last chance to those students. More than 180 students joined the program designed to let every student earn a true high school diploma, while earning college credits with Wayne County Community College and other institutions of higher learning.

THE RESULT

The first class is about to graduate. These students have literally had their lives changed. These young people now have goals they never dreamed of before, such as professional careers, business ownership, and more. The anger has been transferred into enthusiasm for the future. These graduates will be eligible for a CHIP scholarship, as is every child in the Little Rock family.

CONCLUSION

IF PEOPLE'S NEEDS WOULD JUST GO AWAY, I COULD RETIRE

For years I have had people ask me how we at Little Rock can pull off such amazing programs. It really is a matter of faith. We believe we can do these things, so we are able to do them. When I see a problem that exists, I immediately start looking for a solution. I know I am not in this mission alone. I have Jesus and thousands of dedicated helpers.

A wise man once said you can do anything; it is just a matter of engineering it. I believe we can engineer a solution to any problem we face. It is a matter of taking the resources we have and the people we have and combining our efforts creatively to make a project happen. I believe you must give managers latitude to lead and the support they need to achieve the mutual vision. Good people are essential to success. Once you have a system in place with good people managing it with a strong sense of accountability, you can tackle the next problem. The day we are out of problems is the day I can quit.

Appendix 2

Personal Notes

"No Time to Wait, No Time to Lose"

I hope that my research and ideas in this book have challenged you and your community to foster an atmosphere that seeks to improve the economic conditions and future of our people. In addition, I hope I have successfully dispelled the many societal myths surrounding current public opinion, such as:

The poor have too much. However...
- Welfare is down, but poverty is up.
- Usually the last hired are the first laid off.
- Governments continually cut Medicare and insurance coverage for low-income families.
- People in poverty are at a disadvantage when it comes to student loans, job training, and cost-efficient housing.

Even though the preceding truths discount the myth of the poor owning too much, the poor seem to account for the following:
- 9 percent of the Florsheim shoes sales
- 40 percent of music sales in America
- 50 percent of the movie theater ticket revenue
- 36 percent of hair product retail
- 20 percent of Scotch Whiskey consumption

The rich have too little, and yet...
- The rich continue to accumulate wealth and benefit from governmental tax relief.
- 95 percent of American's wealth is owned by 10 percent of the population.

Racism is mighty. However…
- God is almighty.

We have got to do better, ladies and gentlemen. We must break the dependency syndrome. We must eliminate under-developed minds. We must eliminate undisciplined appetites and unethical conduct.

Appendix 3

INSPIRATIONAL SERMON
BY JIM HOLLEY
Building a Case for Black America

God's prescription for reflecting on the past, instruction for the present, and fulfillment of the future can be taken from the Gospel of John. In John's Gospel, Jesus provides us with the prescription for the cure of a sin-sick people that have forgotten the past, are lost in the present, and are directionless regarding their future. Our prescription comes from the fifth chapter of John, which reads:

> After this there was a feast of the Jews; and Jesus went up to Jerusalem. Now there is at Jerusalem by the sheep market a pool, which is called in the Hebrew tongue Bethesda, having five porches. In these lay a great multitude of impotent folk, of blind, halt, withered, waiting for the moving of the water. For an angel went down at a certain season into the pool, and troubled the water: whosoever then first after the troubling of the water stepped in was made whole of whatsoever disease he had. And a certain man was there, which had an infirmity thirty and eight years. When Jesus saw him lie, and knew that he had been now a long time in that case, he saith unto him, Wilt thou be made whole? The impotent man answered him, Sir, I have no man, when the water is troubled, to put me into the pool: but while I am coming, another steppeth down before me. Jesus saith unto him, Rise, take up thy bed, and walk. And immediately the man was made whole, and took up his bed, and walked: and on the same day was the sabbath (vv. 1-9, KJV).

INTRODUCTION

The dog-eat-dog reality of our daily existence has created a chilling atmosphere that makes it difficult to practice compassion. There are numerous examples wherein people have attempted to do a good deed for somebody, only to be betrayed, injured, and in some cases, fatally wounded by the very one they were trying to help.

Recent discussions about welfare fraud and the sad revelation that some monies collected for humanitarian causes went into somebody's pocket rather than toward the elimination of the problem have served to make people more suspicious and distrusting of each other. Where suspicion and distrust abound, there is a reluctance to practice compassion because people are afraid of being exploited or worse. How sad it is that the so-called rotten apples of society have almost spoiled the whole bunch. Certainly there are some people who cheat and exploit every system and situation for their own personal gain. There are those ravenous wolves bedecked in sheep's attire, who know how to capture the attention of others, to manipulate their emotions, and to ensnare those victims in a deadly trap. These sleazy, sinister souls have given needy people and benevolent causes a bum rap. These tricksters are lifted up before the public eye and we are made to believe that everyone who says that they need help is a lazy, lying cheat.

Tragic as it is, there is a growing spirit of selfishness, insensitivity, and callousness when it comes to the matter of practicing compassion for the needy. The age-old affliction of looking out for "number one" has flared up among us. We have drawn tight our purse strings and have taken the attitude that the poor have every day to make it the best way they can. We have probably all heard the expression "You can make it if you try." As inspiring and poetic as it sounds, the raw facts of life dispute the broad application of this truth to any particular situation. There are plenty of people who desperately want to make it with a bull dog's determination or have tried to make it but simply cannot make it on their own. The month outlasts their money. Financial aid eludes them. The job market won't make room for them. Latent skills and abilities have never been brought out in them. So, no matter how diligently they try, there are those who simply can't make it without some help, a hand to lift them up, a voice of inspiration to

65

stir their souls, a strong shoulder to lean on, etc. The quality of life in any society may be determined not by how it treats its rich, able, and affluent but how it treats the weak, struggling, and infirm. When we use this barometer to gauge the depth of our compassion, we cannot help but painfully conclude that the bowels of mercy within us have been closed up and that the springs of sympathy within us have dried up. For there are scores of people that badly need our help, but they are neglected, stepped over, stepped around, and isolated from the mainstream of productive participation in life. No matter how much we pride ourselves on being a civilized and caring race, we have always had a problem practicing compassion for the helpless, which is a part of our past that we have presently forgotten.

We have built our societies for those capable of climbing the corporate ladder, but we make those who lack the ability to climb feel guilty. We even condemn them in our theology by preaching to them that God helps those who help themselves. He is a God of those whom the system has oppressed, suppressed, depressed, and repressed. He is a God that sides with the underdog, not the top dog. He is a God who is a help for the helpless. He causes the lame to walk, the blind to see, the deaf to hear, and the dumb to speak. Nothing disturbed Jesus more in His own day than the suffering of humanity that He witnessed in society. He was particularly appalled at the lack of compassion so evident in the religion of His time. He encountered an unsympathetic religious establishment that demonstrated no concern for the suffering conditions of the people around them. Jesus even became the object of their derision and scorn because He healed on the Sabbath, which they contended was a violation of their sacred laws. These religious leaders displayed a more meticulous regard for the Mosaic Law and the oral traditions than they did for human life. Therefore, we have to be careful, my brothers and sisters, that we don't get so caught up in "having church" that we forget to "be the church." We can become so excited about the formal service that we forget to render service.

When we get right down to it, there is no real worship of God when we fail to serve our fellow man. Religion is useless if it does not make us sensitive to the suffering of others, sympathetic and empathetic with less fortunate, and actively compassionate toward all. There is a need to teach this to our youth. Jesus teaches us this during His visit to the pool of Bethesda, a type of a nursing home or convalescent home located in the heart of the religious capital of the Jewish world. A sense of hopelessness and despair must have greeted the Master as He visited this house of mercy with its five porticoes full of suffering. Based on our knowledge of the reprehensible conditions of some modern nursing care facilities, we can only imagine how loathsome a sight there must have been at this first-century counterpart. The stink of urine and human waste probably was thick in the air. The water in the pool around which the disabled gathered as an object of hope must have been stagnant, and it must have stabbed the human heart with a piercing pain to see human forms lying there amidst this pitiful existence. Around the pool were people who had forgotten that in God we move and have our being. Around this pool were people who in getting what they wanted materially forgot what they had in morals, values, and principles.

John records that a great number of people with illnesses and handicaps were stationed close to the healing waters. Some of these individuals were the impotent, meaning they lacked a basic ability to function in society in any way—no skills, no education, and no hope. Also present were the blind, the lame, and those who were born with a malady or injury that made it impossible for them to secure gainful employment. And, my brothers and sisters, you don't have to go to a nursing home to see these wasting forms today. Drive down the street or look out of your windows and you will see those people seeking our help. These helpless souls are all around us. There were no modern conveniences in Jesus' time. There was no medical staff to attend to the people's conditions. There was no resident social worker to track down their families and keep them abreast of their progress. There were no hospital orderlies to change their bed linens and soiled garments. There was no television, radio, or newspaper to occupy their minds with the latest news. Look at who was around the pool—those who felt that racism is mighty but forgot God is almighty; those who felt that freedom was cheap; those who wanted to break the dependency syndrome; those who have underdeveloped minds, undisciplined appetites, and unethical conduct. Who was there at the pool? Black children who are twice as likely as White children to be born prematurely, suffer low birth weight, or even die during the first year of life; Black children who are born to a teenager or into a single parent family; Black children who are suspended from school or have an unemployed parent; Black children who are three times more likely to be poor, to live in a family headed by a woman, to be assigned to a class for the mentally retarded, to be in foster care, or to die of known child abuse; Black children who are four times as likely to live with neither parent and be supervised in a child welfare agency, to be murdered before the age of one, or to be sent to jail between the ages of 15 and 19; Black children who are five times as likely to be dependent on welfare and become pregnant as teenagers; and Black children who are twelve times as likely to live with a parent who never married—only four out of ten Black children now live in a two-parent family. It is a sad reality that we see Black men in welfare lines, Black women in ADC lines, Black boys in drug lines, and Black girls in pregnancy lines.

This situation essentially guarantees the poverty of Black children for the foreseeable future. Well, these type of people were wasting away around the pool at Bethesda. The only hope of a cure for their affliction was the pool, which legend said was stirred once a year by a descending angel. The angel was said to fill the water with healing properties for the first person who managed to step in during this moment. However, these people, much like us, forgot God's amazing power. Tell your children how God watched over the slaves. Tell your children how God delivered them off the plantations. Tell your children how God helped our fore-parents build institutions of higher learning, such as Tuskegee, Clark, Shaw, and Fisk. Tell your children that in such a short time, we have become presidential candidates, mayors, lieutenant governors, and members of Congress. Tell your children how the Lord God brought the Israelites into the land of milk and honey. Tell your children how God blessed them with immeasurably good things. Tell your children we must not worship other gods, such as the gods of drugs, crime, abortion, apathy, docility, drunkenness, unethical conduct, and undisciplined appetites.

A CHALLENGE FOR OUR PEOPLE

This man had blamed others for his condition. "While I am coming, another steppeth down before me." Jesus said, "Walk man! Nobody is obligated to let you go first. Everybody around here is seeking help, just like you. They don't have to abandon their hope, just for you." My brethren, be trusting enough to obey Jesus! Be strong enough to stand up on your own! Walk, and you won't have to depend on anybody to carry you! Walk, and you can go where you want to go and do what you want to do! Walk, Black Man! Walk!

Don't be afraid and insecure. Try your legs, and do something for yourself! Walk! We need to go back to the old ways of loving everybody! Let's teach our children to say, "Yes, ma'am" and "No, sir." Let's respect each other, including our elders. Let's do unto others as we would have others to do unto us. Let's restore the extended family. We need to teach our kids to stop wearing $40 hats on a ten cent head. Likewise, we should instruct our kids to stop wearing $80 shoes because that is too much money to walk around on. Let's teach our girls to be more concerned about books and less concerned about their bosoms. We need to teach our boys to be men of God. With men walking around with curlers in their head, bags on their heads, or earrings in their ears, the children can't tell if they have two mamas. Daddy is in the beauty shop; mama is in the beauty shop. Daddy is wearing silk underwear; mama is wearing silk underwear. We need a revival. We need to go to church school. We need to go to Baptist Training Union. We need to go to the National Baptist Congress. We need to go to prayer meetings. We need to go to Bible class. As the song says, "Get right church, and let's go home."

CONCLUSION

The man looked up at Jesus, and he felt a stirring in his soul. Nobody had ever attempted to help this man by inspiring him to stand and walk on his own. He felt his bed sores dry up. His withered legs were enfleshed with life. His ankles and bones received strength. For the first time in thirty-eight years, he stood up by the power of God and took a step. Hallelujah! Watch him! He wobbled at first and almost lost his balance. However, hope got under one arm, while faith took him by the other arm. Love got in one leg, and grace got in the other leg. He took a second step, and the third one came easily. Jesus empowered and enabled this man even in his deficiency. My brothers and sisters, we have consumer power. We have voting power. But more importantly, we have God's power and that's enough! Didn't you read, "Blessed is the man that walketh not in the counsel of the ungodly, nor standeth in the way of sinners, nor sitteth in the seat of the scornful" (Ps. 1:1, KJV)? Or what about, "The earth is the LORD's and the fulness thereof" (Ps. 24:1, KJV)? Don't you remember when David said, "The LORD is my shepherd; I shall not want" (Ps. 23:1, KJV)? Or when he said, "The LORD is my light and my salvation; whom shall I fear? the LORD is the strength of my life; of whom shall I be afraid" (Ps. 27:1, KJV)? Or when he said, "Fret not thyself because of evildoers, neither be thou envious against the workers of iniquity" (Ps. 37:1, KJV)? Didn't you hear Jesus say, "Let not your heart be troubled" (John 14:1, KJV)? Didn't you hear His disciple John say, "Beloved, I wish above all things that thou mayest prosper and be in health, even as thy soul prospereth" (3 John 2, KJV)? Didn't you hear the TV commercials talk about Him? If you say Coke, He's the real thing. If you say Pepsi, Jesus can make you come alive. If you say Maxwell House Coffee™, Jesus is good to the last drop. If you say He's like a Timex watch, He'll take a licking and keep on ticking. If you say He's like Scotch® Tape, you can't see Him, but you know He's there. If you say He's like Allstate, you are in good hands. If you say He's like Prudential, He's like the rock. He is like Tide™—He'll get all of the dirt out. My brothers and sisters, it doesn't matter how long you've been down. If you're willing, God is able! Jesus is the help for the helpless, the hope for the hopeless, and the way for the wandering. He is a light in a dark place, sure footing on shaky ground, and a solid rock beneath faltering feet. Jesus can help you no matter what you are facing today!

In closing, all I know is school informed me, sin deformed me, but thanks be to God, Jesus transformed me. When I was a child, I read nursery rhymes. I read about Jack and Jill who went up a hill to fetch a pail of water. Jack fell down and broke his crown, and Jill came tumbling after. Don't expect people to do for you what you can do for yourself! There is not a White man smart enough to do to us what we are doing to ourselves. Remember, we have consumer power. We must use our economic influence. Black Americans have $250 billion in disposable income. Black America does three times more trade with corporate America than Russia, China, Japan, and West Germany combined.

Capitalism, communism, and socialism are the dominant economic ideologies in the world today. Globalism is the ideology that transcends all the rest. Our sights must shift from charity to parity, from aid to trade, from social generosity to economic reciprocity, from welfare to our share. We spent $2 billion-plus yet owe 2 percent less than 12 percent of the population. However, we eat 18 percent of the rice. We drink 20 percent of the orange juice. We buy 28 percent of the Dalgeish Cadillacs. We buy 9 percent of the Florsheim shoes. We buy 40 percent of the records in America. We buy 50 percent of the movie tickets. We buy 36 percent of the hair products. We are 13 percent of the population, but drink 20 percent of the Scotch Whiskey. If you took Blacks out of America, Wall Street would suddenly collapse.

The man in John 5 used superstition as an excuse. He was waiting on an angel to come down in that pool and stir the water. Now after 38 years, this man had not seen any angel come down and do anything. It was all superstition. That false expectation was the only hope those sick people had, yet there was no truth in it. In today's society, some people have placed their hope in superstitions. They put their hope in roots, rabbit's feet, lucky charms, horseshoes, the zodiac, and almanacs. I am so amazed by how many college students are depending on osmosis for graduation. Put your hope in something real! Put your hope in Jesus! Some people can't start the day until they read their horoscope. Your condition is not determined by the chance position of a star. Some people stand around all day listening for recurring numbers. Your condition is not determined by a number. We can even use the Bible as a good luck charm. We don't read it for truth to live by, but we carry one around to ward off evil spirits and bring us good luck. My brothers and sisters, no angel descends and conjures up any position. There is no hocus-pocus about life. There's no magic! It takes faith, fortitude, grit, grace, divine help, and human determination. We must build our hope on things eternal. We must hold to God's unchanging hand. Let's learn some new four letter words: work, nice, kind, good, and grit.

Another excuse this man used was that of blaming others for his failure. He said, "While I am coming, another steppeth down before me" (v. 7, KJV). Basically he was saying, "I could have been healed a long time ago, but every time I get ready to get in the water somebody jumps in front of me and gets in first." The truth of the matter is, this man hadn't done much to help himself. He had resigned himself to his situation and decided to blame his failure on everybody else. Racism is not responsible for us killing each other—it's us! Racism is not responsible for the condition of our school system—it's us! The statistics show our youth are selling drugs, conceiving children out of wedlock, and dropping out of school more than any other ethnic group. However, it's not because of racism—it's you! You are not failing at your job because your boss doesn't like you—it's you! You did not get a below average grade because your teacher has something against you—you didn't do the work!

It's you! It's you! It's you!

We're always standing around blaming our failures on somebody else when in reality we haven't done all we could do to improve ourselves! Jesus asked the man, "Wilt thou be made whole?" (v. 6, KJV) and the man started giving excuses that were designed to make Jesus feel sorry for him. You have got to look out because some people use their condition to elicit sympathy yet have no intentions of trying to do better. The Mormons have Utah, and they have no intentions of giving it back to America. We debate about Black colleges. Jews don't debate about Brandeis University. Catholics don't debate whether or not to support Notre Dame. With $200 billion dollars, we spend 6.6 percent with other Blacks. We spend almost 95 percent with non-Blacks. We spend 95 percent of our money with groups that spend 5 percent with us. We give our money to others so they will like us. When we spend our money on products produced by African Americans it is called "segregation," while other ethnic groups call it "profit." We are too busy being a minority and being poor. Poverty for us is now an art form. If you want anything or have anything, we call upon you to apologize for having something.

Look at us politically: we have political power. Blacks have 17 million eligible voters, but only 10 million are registered. Six and a half million African Americans voted in the presidential election of 2004 but seven million still remain unregistered. In 2004, Bush's victory margin in Alabama was 17,462, but 250,349 Black voters were unregistered. Arkansas was a similar story—the victory margin for Bush was 5,123, while unregistered Blacks in the state numbered 109,348. In Tennessee, the margin was 4,710, while the number of unregistered Blacks was 208,553. In other words, Bush should never have been president in the first place.

Let me tell you, Blacks can make a difference. Jesse Jackson is making a difference. Politics in America will never be the same. America plays games. We can pick cotton. We can cut tobacco. We can be slaves in our labor, and we can die. Even though Barack Obama is making a difference, it remains to be seen if an African American can be president.

Bibliography

Bonhoeffer, Dietrich. *The Cost of Discipleship*. New York: Macmillan Publishing Co., 1963.

Cone, James H. "Black Theology in American Religion." *Journal of the American Academy of Religion 8*. (Spring 1985): 179-201.

Felton, Carroll M., Jr. *The Care of Souls in the Black Church: A Liberation Perspective*. New York: Martin Luther King Fellows Press, 1980.

Fraser, George C. *Race for Success: The Ten Best Business Opportunities for Blacks in America*. New York: William Morrow and Co., 1998.

Hutchinson, Earl Ofari. *The Crisis in Black and Black*. Los Angeles: Middle Passage Press, 1998.

Kehrein, Glen and Raleigh Washington. *Breaking Down the Walls: A Model for Reconciliation in an Age of Racial Strife*. Chicago: Moody Press, 1993.

Lincoln, C. Eric and Lawrence H. Mamiya. *The Black Church in the African American Experience*. Durham, NC: Duke University Press, 1990.

Makechnie, George K. *Howard Thurman: His Enduring Dream*. Boston: Boston University Press, 1988.

Pannell, William. *Evangelism From the Bottom Up*. Grand Rapids: Zondervan Publishing House, 1992.

Perkins, John M. *Beyond Charity: The Call to Christian Community Development*. Grand Rapids: Baker Book House, 1993.

_____. *A Quiet Revolution: The Christian Response to Human Need, a Strategy for Today.* Pasadena, CA: Urban Family Publications, 1996.

_____, ed. *Restoring At-Risk Communities: Doing It Together and Doing It Right.* Grand Rapids: Baker Book House, 1996.

Rivers, Eugene F. "On the Responsibility of Intellectuals in the Age of Crack." *Boston Review,* September-October (1992).

Stott, John R. W. *Christian Mission in the Modern World.* Downers Grove, IL: InterVarsity Press, 1975.

Thurman, Howard. *The Search for Common Ground. An Inquiry into the Basis of Man's Experience of Community.* Richmond, IN: Friends United Press, 1986.

Vanzant, Iyanla. *Acts of Faith: Daily Meditations for People of Color.* New York: Simon and Schuster, 1996.

Venable, Abraham S. *Building Black Business: An Analysis and a Plan.* New York: Earl Graves Publishing, 1972.

Welch, Severson. To Reverend Jim Holley, 23 November 1994. Transcript in the hand of Rev. Jim Holley. Personal letter.

West, Cornel. *Prophesy Deliverance!: An Afro-American Revolutionary Christianity.* Philadelphia: Westminster John Knox Press, 1982.

Wilder, L. Douglas written to the Economic Club of Detroit. Detroit, March 17, 1992.

Wilmore, Gayraud S. and James H. Cone, eds. *Black Theology: A Documentary History.* Marymoll, NY: Orbis Books, 1979.

Printed in the United States
202398BV00002B/1-315/P